MATTHEW ARNOLD
and 'Thyrsis'

Patrick Carill Connolly

GREENWICH EXCHANGE
LONDON

Greenwich Exchange, London

First published in Great Britain in 2004
All rights reserved

Printed and bound by Q3 Digital/Litho, Loughborough
Tel: 01509 213456
Typesetting and layout by Albion Associates, London
Tel: 020 8852 4646
Cover design by December Publications, Belfast
Tel: 028 90286559

Cover: Detail from 'In the vale of Amersham' by Alfred Vickers
PHOTOGRAPH REPRODUCED WITH THE KIND PERMISSION OF THE
TRUSTEES OF THE MUSEUMS & GALLERIES OF NORTHERN IRELAND

Greenwich Exchange Website: www.greenex.co.uk
ISBN 1-87155-61-7

To Sarah and Malcolm, who kept faith.

Contents

Author's Foreword

Arnold was a bit of a dandy with a laconic even self-deprecating sense of humour. This deadpanness, that came unconsciously of having to hide his childhood feelings, often caused him to be misinterpreted as aloof if not patronising, and has not helped his reputation as either poet or critic. Indeed, it has helped further the accusation of elitism against him.

As a critic he set himself the huge task (and monumental task, as both privately and proudly he knew) of trying to isolate what, in the Western tradition, had been regarded as aesthetically pleasing and thereby to build and universalise a system of aesthetic judgement applicable to all literature in all ages.

Such a system was bound to be monolithic and by its nature (i.e. in terms of 19th century European notions of moral superiority and progress) would exclude other traditions both inside and outside the West. Any universal critique is fated to become a tyrant of form, and we may be reminded of Stalin's attack on Shostakovitch's work as being "formalist" and not conforming to the artistic demands of socialist realism.

Because of this unifying attempt, and the grounds and choice of his selection (and his being a Victorian further tended to bias 20th century judgements of him), he was perceived as being an aesthetic elitist. But Arnold injected spirituality into the notion of culture, the sweetness and light – as he believed – that can lead to human perfection. To repeat his oft-quoted statement (from *Literature and Dogma,* 1873), culture is "the acquainting ourselves with the best that has been known and said in the world, and thus with the history of the human spirit."

Arnold's argument that criticism should extract the best from human culture as a benchmark for aesthetic judgement has to many implied that there was a group or class or nation that had or should have a monopoly on it. But Arnold says no such thing – after all, aristocrats he dismissed as Barbarians (with their love of war, epic, honour and whores), the middle class as Philistines (land-grabbing, mercantile and Mammonite) and the lower classes as the Populace (anarchic, shifting, drunken, selfish). His aim was to draw all towards perfection, and there was a good reason for this: as he wrote to his sister Fan, the benefits of the new state education would be seen in "civilising" the working class, who, he believed, would soon be the dominant political force in Britain. Note that he chooses *civilising,* not *educating.* Education, especially state education, bore the possibility of bias and political indoctrination. His concern was to give the highest standards to this new majority, to teach them to consider and question, not regurgitate, outdated tenets. This is hardly the position of an elitist, unless we define elitism as exclusivity or standards as social discrimination. That position was left to 20th century cultural analysts, each in pursuit of their own convictions, such as F.R. Leavis of the traditionalist-moralist movement, Allan Bloom the American individualist-capitalist, and the members of the marxist 'Frankfurt School,' all of whom positively disliked the notion of making culture populist.

Today mainstream cultural criticism appears to have bogged itself down in the politics of egalitarianism and the creation of a semantics to express it. Inevitably cultural critics alienate themselves from the society they are trying to educate (let alone civilise), turning on its head Arnold's dictum that critical language should be plain if it is not to fall into the pit of semantically disguised prejudice. Or New Age obscurantism, as the critic Slavoj Zizek puts it.

Ironically, the egalitarian culturalists have become today's elitists, armchaired in their middle-class-liberal pastime of pontificating to the masses. It seems the poor old working class just can't be left alone, especially by those of a liberal socialist persuasion. And far from being drawn into culture – however that may be defined (usually politically or sociologically, and often with spectacular infights a Swift couldn't better) – the working class is driven back into the laager of its old beliefs to defend itself against what is perceives as cultural genocide. Where Huxley argued for a culture composed of rational truth and material practicality, we appear nowadays to live in a culture of ideological truth and material dependence. The spirituality Arnold saw as the heart of culture, crucial to civilised man, has been ripped out of it, and criticism is left groping for some mechanical replacement.

To the satisfaction of his detractors, Arnold the poet is seen as failing his own critical tests, thus disproving his own poetics. The assumption is then made that he came to believe himself a poetic failure and turned against his own bent by becoming a critic. And certainly if we wish to find fault in Arnold's poetry we will, as indeed we can in Homer's or Shakespeare's. The simple truth is that emotionally he was inclined to the Romantic, but aesthetically disliked its structural and formal looseness. This is one reason he evades making a judgemental critique of Romantic poets in 'The Study of Poetry' (from *Essays in Criticism*, 1888), self-excusingly describing such an attempt as stepping on "burning ground." If any simple judgement of his poetry should be made it is perhaps that he tried to bridge the gap between Romanticism and Classicism, between emotion and proportion, between the picturesque or decorative and their structural objective.

It is a commonplace that each generation questions the relevance of the past – aesthetic and political as well as historical – to the here and now. Arnold is no exception to this, either as critic or poet. I have already noted how his criticism is seen as outdated, and to those of a political bent even distasteful. His poetry has suffered not by adverse reaction but simply by being ignored, as if a disgraced critic must have written disgraceful poetry. And the progression since the First World War has been a slow but steady diminishing of Arnold's work to something approaching irrelevancy: "He also wrote poems," as an article on *The Guardian* website says dismissively.[1]

But the relevance of one thing to another, of how one thing bears on another, whether past to present or this mode to that, is self-enclosed. How does a Hannibal bear on a Congreve, save in the use the one makes of the other, and in aesthetic terms this use has to be by the latter on the former. Irrelevance will not make the former redundant, nor will later relevance make the former suddenly and often falsely important as if it had only existed to be appreciated by the future. As far as I am aware Hannibal's life had no influence on – no relevance to Congreve's choice of dramatic subject matter. So what? – asks a classicist or archaeologist or military strategist. Hannibal and Congreve inhabited worlds as separate as that of the apple to the pear. The question should rather ask the relevance of past actions and attitudes to those they have in common with the present, where their parameters overlay each other, otherwise the comparison becomes the ridiculous analogue of a bad simile. The relevance of relevancy is how the past dealt with problems we still experience today. And as Arnold saw, it is human spirituality that gives relevancy its wherefore.

Poets supposedly killed off as irrelevant for whatever reason by one generation (Milton by Eliot, Tennyson by the Georgians) bounce back at the next rebellious mindset, perhaps proving Arnold's belief in the judgement of monumentality. This resurrection of the old by the new may be expressive of generational conflict or academic self-furtherance but at least our awareness becomes expanded. The reasoning behind the relevance may be wrong but the empathy is right – we need to feel that humanity past and to come shares the same passions and fears as ourselves, the need for constancy amidst change. Relevancy depends, however, not only on the present and external but on the internal realities. What is relevant to a 19th century sociologist is not to a 20th century one. Both are irrelevant to a Buddhist. And we can ask of what political or economic or moral or social use to anyone is Coleridge's 'Kubla Khan'? The answer is none. The answer is also that the poem gives us aesthetic pleasure, induced by the mythopoeic world it draws us into. But when poetry concerns itself with purely rational concepts it has dropped out of the mythopoeic, out of its own reality, into the world of prejudicial versifying. Relevance in such cases has gone beyond its own parameters. 'Kubla Khan' – or any poem that bewitches us – appeals to the inner world of our own individuality, a world beyond the pressure and evanescence of the mundane.

Poetry inhabits its own world, and not only differs in its effect upon but in its visualisation within the individual mind. The evocation of a poem is unique to the reader. We extract from a poem what appeals to our personal experience, personal expectation, to our personal tastes, and though elements of these may be common to our humanity our enjoyment and appreciation lie in our individual approach to the poem and its guiding of our journey through the mythopoeic reality it has produced in our mind.

Arnold sought to analyse what aesthetically and spiritually is common to our humanity in order to find a broad ground on which to base acceptable cultural standards. Although he attempted to apply his findings to his own poetic creations it is generally recognised that he succeeds only when he ignores his own aesthetic strictures. It is the worlds he created in short poems like 'Requiescat' or longer ones like 'The Scholar-Gypsy' and 'Dover Beach' – with their delicate balance between melancholy and its structural expression – that first attracted me to Arnold. It was his talent (once he allowed himself to unfetter it) for yoking the reader without any seeming effort on his or our part to the world of his poetic imagination, and allowing us the freedom to roam within it, that I found especially refreshing. This accessibility, this ease with which he can draw us into his world, makes him the lazy man's poet.

His verbal restraint amidst an intuitive handling of emotion and symbolism shows itself above all in 'Thyrsis'. The reasons will be found in this essay and I have structured it to lead up to an analysis not just of the poem but of why I personally am so partial to it, in the hope that my partiality will enthuse others to read Arnold not as a cultural or scholastic duty but as a personal pleasure. If so, then I trust that my effort won't be judged as just another critique with its own cultural axe to grind, and that any question of Arnold's relevance in whatever form, critical poetic or otherwise, to the here and now becomes itself irrelevant.

Footnote

[1] *The Bluffer's Guide to Culture Buffs* (and not as a tongue-in-cheek comment either).

Chronology:
Arnold and the Victorians'
"Main Movement of Mind"

24th December 1822 – The birth of Matthew Arnold at Laleham-on-Thames, near Staines, the eldest son of Dr Thomas Arnold (born 1795) and Mary Penrose (born 1791), who ran a small private school at Laleham. Shelley had drowned earlier that year.

23rd January 1823 – Matthew was christened, one of his godfathers being John Keble, a friend of Dr Arnold, though later the two would fall out. Death of David Ricardo, economist, whose theory that labour determines value was to greatly influence Marx's *Das Kapital* of 1867. In the summer of 1824 Matthew's legs were put in iron-braces to counteract the crookedness of his legs (due to rickets?). He was shackled to them for two years.

1826 – The death of Byron impelled a sluggish British government to espouse the cause of Greek liberation, culminating in the sinking of the Turkish fleet in Navarino Bay in 1827. The first Burmese war came to an end.

1828 – Dr Arnold, a man strong in his own morality, was appointed headmaster of Rugby School. Matthew attended school at Laleham, then with his brother Tom was taught by private tutor.

1830 – Opening of the Liverpool and Manchester Railway by the Duke of Wellington.

1831 – Michael Faraday invented the dynamo.

1832 – Poems by Tennyson, including 'The Lady of Shalott' and 'Marianne'. Death of Sir Walter Scott. George Sand's *Valentine*, a novel of free love.

1833 – *Principles of Geology* by Charles Lyell. Ralph Waldo Emerson toured England, meeting Wordsworth, Carlyle and Coleridge. Death of Trevithick, pioneer of steam locomotion.

The Arnolds had visited the Lakes in 1831 when Matthew was eight, and became friends with Wordsworth. He wrote to the Doctor in 1832 informing him that suitable land was for sale near Rydal between Grasmere and Ambleside. Fox Howe house was built in 1834, Wordsworth helping with its design, and he continued to visit the Arnolds there till his death in 1850. Fox Howe was a retreat for Arnold throughout his life even if "he rubbed up against its customary sobriety, with his irrepressible vivacity" as Nicholas Murray (to whom I am much indebted for the details of Arnold's life) says in his *A Life of Matthew Arnold*, 1996.

1836 – Arnold attended Winchester College. *Utilitarianism* by John Stuart Mill, an empirical work which based knowledge on experience and reason.

1837 – Arnold was enrolled at Rugby School in August 1837, just as a certain Arthur Hugh Clough was leaving it for Oxford. Dickens serialised *Pickwick Papers* and *Oliver Twist*. In 1838 Brunel's *The Great Western* became the first screwdriven iron steamship to cross the Atlantic. Thomas Carlyle's *The French Revolution, A History*.

1839 – The first electric telegraph line was opened between Paddington and West Drayton. The first of the two Opium Wars with China started. Talbot and Daguerre publicise the progress of their separate experiments in photography. At Rugby Matthew became friends with Thomas Hughes, but was not a promising scholar: "I do not see how the sources of deep thought are to be reached in him" wrote his father, worried about Matthew's seeming frivolity. Despite his father's misapprehensions Matthew won an open scholarship to Balliol College, Oxford in 1840.

1841 – *On Heroes, Hero-Worship, and The Heroic in History* by Carlyle, which attributed the advance in human culture to the actions of great leaders. At Oxford Arnold's closest companions were his brother Tom and Arthur Clough. They shared walks in the hills about Oxford. Emerson's *Essays*.

George Sand, Emerson and Carlyle were especial influences on Arnold at this time, and these resulted in a loosening of his Christian faith. In Sand, Arnold found a kindred spirit of revolt and an attempt to purify human society, though her sexual freedom he found somewhat disturbing. Emerson's influence on Arnold lay in his use of oratory and rhetoric, but Arnold had misgivings about his agnostic philosophy and his poetic abilities which he considered not plain and concrete enough. Goethe was another influence for his "profound, imperturbable naturalism" and jolting appeal to modernity that loosened "routine thinking".

1842 – *Poems in Two Volumes* by Tennyson. *Dramatic Lyrics* by Browning, including 'My Last Duchess'. On the 12th June Dr Arnold died aged 46 of angina. Matthew was warned that he might die early of a similar cause. His mother and his unmarried sister Frances ('Fan') retired to Fox Howe.

1843 – Ruskin published *Modern Painters*. The first Opium War ended. *A Christmas Carol* by Dickens.

1844 – Joseph Turner foreshadowed Impressionism with his *Rain, Steam and Speed*. In November Arnold gained a 2nd class degree and became a temporary master at Rugby until he gained a fellowship at Oriel College, Oxford in March 1845. Browning published *Dramatic Romances and Lyrics*, including 'Home-Thoughts from Abroad'.

1846 – Free trade triumphed with the repeal of the corn laws. Height of the Irish potato famine. Arnold visited George Sand in France.

1847 – *Jane Eyre*, *Agnes Grey* and *Wuthering Heights* by Charlotte, Anne and Emily Bronte. In April (until 1851) Arnold became private secretary to Lord Lansdowne, a Whig marquis who was president of the privy Council and responsible for matters of state relating to education. A dull but honourable aristocrat, says Murray, he liked nothing better than helping people to a position befitting them. 'The Princess' by Tennyson. Matthew's brother William joined the Bengal Army of the East India Company in February 1848 and in September

Arnold visited Thun in Switzerland where – it appears – he had an affair with a girl he calls Marguerite. Thackeray serialised *Vanity Fair*.

1848 – The year of revolutions in Europe. J.S. Mill's *Principles of Political Economy*, *Dombey and Sons* by Dickens, *The Tenant of Wildfell Hall* by Anne Bronte. Her sister Emily died of tuberculosis, as did Anne and their brother Branwell the following year. Rossetti formed the Pre-Raphaelite Brotherhood with Millais and Hunt. Elizabeth ('Mrs') Gaskell published *Mary Barton*.

On the 26th February 1849 Arnold published *The Strayed Reveller and Other Poems*. Later that year he started courting Fanny (or Flu, as he called her) Lucy Wightman, a judge's daughter, described by a contemporary as a "zealous High Churchwoman of the Tractarian School", almost the opposite to Marguerite. In 1849 also appeared John Ruskin's *The Seven Lamps of Architecture* that – with *The Stones of Venice* – worked towards the Tractarian theory that the high point of Western architecture was to be found in Gothic art. Such art, as opposed to the aesthetic drabness of contemporary industrial buildings, was perceived as being driven by a spiritual not material commitment.

1850 – Wordsworth died. Tennyson became Poet Laureate and published *In Memoriam*, an elegy for his friend Arthur Hallam. *David Copperfield* by Dickens.

1851 – The Great Exhibiton. Death of Joseph Turner RA. In April Lord Lansdowne appointed Arnold as an inspector of schools.

1852 – Death of Wellington. Arnold's second volume of poetry *Empedocles on Etna and other Poems, by A* appeared in October. This contained 'Memorial Verses', most of the Marguerite poems, the 'Faded Leaves' sequence, and 'Tristram and Iseult'. The second Burmese war.

November 1853 – *Poems: A New Edition* was published, his third volume of poetry. Instead of "By A" it carried his name. It contained a preface, 'Sohrab and Rustum', 'The Scholar-Gypsy' and other poems. *Cranford* by Mrs Gaskell. In 1854 Arnold's *General Inspection Report* was published – he asked for such reports to be "unvarnished and literal", and such a prosaic style – untrammelled by stylistic regulations – he felt would release him from the artistic constraints he imposed on his own poetry.

December 1854 – *Poems by Matthew Arnold, Second Series*, a reprint of earlier poems with the addition of 'Balder Dead'. *Hard Times* by Dickens.

1855 – *Maud: A Monodrama* by Tennyson. *Men and Women* by Browning, including 'Fra Lippo Lippi' and 'Childe Roland to the Dark Tower Came'. *North and South* by Mrs Gaskell. Her friend Charlotte Bronte died during pregnancy. On the 12th June Clough married Blanche Smith, a cousin of Florence Nightingale. The Crimean War was now raging (1853-6). Arnold published *Poems – Second Series* which included 'Balder Dead'. In August he took out a lease on a house in Grosvenor Street West and the family was freed from their wandering life of living in boarding houses, hotels and with family. On 14th November his son Dick was born. In February 1856 he was elected to membership of the Athenaeum Club in Piccadilly, whose library he was to make great use of and many of his letters and articles would be written here. His portrait by Weigall still hangs there.

1857 – *On the Modern Element in Literature*. From 1857 to 1867 Arnold served two consecutive terms at Oxford as Professor of Poetry. His idea of the lectures was to "establish a formula which shall sort all literature". He again visited the Continent but without his family.

1858 – The Great Stink of London, when the Thames' stench drove Parliament to instruct Sir Joseph Bazelgette to construct an efficient sewage system and pumping stations to cope with the city's effluent problems. As a result of the Indian Mutiny of the previous year, the Act for the Better Government of India was passed whereby the East India Company's governmental responsibilities were transferred to the Crown. On the 25th December Arnold's daughter Lucy was born.

1859 – Darwin published *On The Origin Of Species*; J.S. Mill published *On Liberty*; the contrast between them is enlightening.

On the 9th April Arnold's brother Willy died in Gibraltar en route from India. In August the family again holidayed in Dover. 1859 to 1885 – Tennyson working on *Idylls of the King*. The prose work *England and the Italian Question* (the question being the possible conflict of Austria and France over Sardinia, which was trying to oust Austria from the Italian mainland) had been published while the Arnolds were in Dover, and was more concerned with the intrenchedness of the English ruling classes than with France's possible violation of the treaty of Vienna. Arnold was confident that political change – "the triumph of the modern spirit" – was inevitable.

1860 – The British took Peking at the end of the second Opium War. General Gordon burned down the Summer Palace. Arnold's poems written about this time included two on the death of his brother Willy – 'Stanzas from Carnac' and 'A Southern Night', both highlighting the difference between the languid climes of the south and the workaday industrialisation of the north, mirroring Arnold's emotional duality – the cold formality of England fighting the indolence and romantic ambience of the Mediterranean. The poems were published in 1867.

1861 – *Popular Education in France*. On the 13th November Clough died in Florence. Arnold promised his widow that among the Cumner Hills they had trod in their youth "I shall be able to think him over as I could wish". Robert Browning came to one Sunday lunch, and was described by Arnold as a "remarkably agreeable converser" (he also thought him "a man with a moderate gift"). He was writing many essays at this time and published *On Translating Homer* (1861 – 2). *Great Expectations* by Dickens.

November 1862 – *Heine's Grave* (Arnold had previously lectured on the German poet), an attack on the philistinism of English culture, excused by Heine's contempt for English attitudes.

1864 – Brunel built the Clifton Suspension Bridge. Gordon put down the Taiping rebellion, earning himself the nickname 'Chinese' Gordon. *Dramatis Personae* by Browning, including 'Caliban upon Setebos'. In January 1864 Arnold met Disraeli who had written novels about industrial life but had given up writing because, as Arnold said, he could not do two things at once. Tennyson's 'Enoch Arden' appeared – "I do not think Tennyson a great and powerful spirit in any line."

1865 – *Essays in Criticism* (first edition – the second was published shortly after his death in 1888). Death of Elizabeth Gaskell. *Researches into the Early History of Mankind* by the anthropologist Sir Edward Burnett. The end of the American civil war.

July 1866 – The *Pall Mall Gazette* published the first of Arnold's comic letters concerning Baron von Thunder-Ten-Tronkh, later collected in *Friendship's Garland* of 1871. The Great Eastern laid the first successful transatlantic cable.

19th August 1866 – the birth of Basil, his last child. His last lecture as Professor of Poetry was given on 26th May 1866 (*The Celtic Element in English Poetry*). During this period he met and befriended the Darwinian Thomas Huxley, though they had their disagreements.

1867 – Arnold published *On the Study of Celtic Literature* and *New Poems* (though few of them were). 'Empedocles on Etna' was included at the urging of Swinburne and Browning. Besides those written some years before the new poems included 'The Terrace at Berne', 'Dover Beach', 'Rugby Chapel', 'Calais Sands', 'Growing Old', 'Oberman Once More' and a number of sonnets including the 'Rachel' group. The Abyssinian war, in which the British Museum acquired 400 Ethiopic manuscripts whose ownership is still in dispute.

1868 – A terrible year for the Arnolds: on 11th January their youngest child Basil died, and on 23rd November their eldest son Thomas also died.

1869 – *Culture and Anarchy* (revised in 1875). In June the two-volume collected edition of his poems appeared; the first volume was entitled *Narrative and Elegiac*, the second *Dramatic and Lyric*. There were no new poems. In this year appeared Browning's *The Ring and the Book*. The teenage Prince Thomas of Savoy lodged with the Arnolds.

1871 – *Friendship's Garland* published. A collection of satirical essays attacking the English lack of intellectualism and their belief in "blind custom and prejudice", told through the mouthpiece of Arminius von Thunder-ten-Tronkh, a Prussian. Later editions included the 1866 article 'My Countrymen'. Believers in science were not treated respectfully and the English middle class, "drugged with business", was contrasted with the Europeans and their intellectual liberality. George Eliot (Mary Ann Evans) serialised *Middlemarch*. The physicist James Maxwell published *Theory of Heat*. The Franco-Prussian War ended.

1873 – *Literature and Dogma*. Death of John Stuart Mill. *Studies in the History of the Renaissance* by Walter Pater, where 'Art for art's sake' was first promulgated and became the artistic touchstone for aestheticists such as Oscar Wilde in the 1880s. James Maxwell's *Treatise on Electricity and Magnetism*.

1875 – The revised edition of *Culture and Anarchy* appeared.

1879 – *Mixed Essays*. The Zulu War, the battles of Isandhlawana and Rorke's Drift. *The Europeans* by Henry James. 1878-80 William Morris composed 'The Earthly Paradise'. 'Dramatic Idylls' by Browning appeared in the following year.

1881 – Arnold had his portrait painted by George Frederick Watts for the Royal Academy exhibition. The first Boer War. The British were defeated at Majuba and the Transvaal gained its independence. *The Portrait of a Lady* by Henry James.

January 1882 – the poem 'Westminster Abbey' published on the occasion of Dean Arthur Stanley's death, a defence of a broad liberal church instead of one "grown strait in soul". In March appeared *Irish Essays* (three essays and a preface) concerning the "need of a changed and more attractive power in English civilisation". The novelist Amelia Edwards founded the Egypt Exploration Fund. Arnold's son Dick returned from Australia and was appointed an Inspector of Factories in Manchester. In October he decided to retire, thinking because of *Literature and Dogma* that Gladstone would not promote him. However, in August 1883 he was offered a civil list pension of

£250 a year in recognition of his services to poetry and literature. The death of Rossetti.

October 1883 to March 1884 – Arnold, Flu and daughter Lucy sailed to America for his lecture tour. In April 1884 his son Dick had married Ella Ford. Arnold noted she would not make his son richer. The Mahdi rebellion in the Sudan. In December Lucy married Frederick Whitridge, an American lawyer she had met in New York.

January 1885 – General Gordon was killed two days before a British column relieved Khartoum. Arnold was again offered the Professorship of Poetry at Oxford but declined. *Discourses in America* published. Mandalay fell to the British. In November Arnold started his third foreign schools mission. He went to Berlin and heard Bismark speak, "a bad, untrained speaker … keeps his head down, does not speak out" – an ironic description of his own faults perhaps, after the experience of his American lecture tour. He also had a private audience with the Kaiser. He returned home for Christmas.

January 1886 – Arnold set off again on his mission, firstly to Paris then Nuremberg, Munich and Switzerland. He attended Wagner's *Tristan and Isolde* (Arnold too had composed a poem on the lovers) and described the second act as "without any action". "I have managed the story better than Wagner" he wrote to Flu. Unfortunately his public did not think so. On the 22nd May Arnold, Flu and Nelly set off for America from Liverpool. They were met at New York by Lucy and her daughter. He visited Massachusetts, Chicago, the Niagara Falls and Philadelphia. He criticised American life as "uninteresting, so without savour and without depth", with newspapers of "badness and ignobleness". Ominously his heart gave him trouble while bathing. They returned to Liverpool on 13th September.

12th November 1886 – Arnold retired and was presented with a silver claret jug and salver. To the cheers of the guests he said: "to the government I owe nothing".

14th April 1888 – Arnold went with Flu to Liverpool to meet Lucy and Fred, staying with his brother-in-law John Cropper, a Liverpool businessman and philanthropist living in Dingle, whose house a visitor reported was "impregnated with holiness". The next day, while walking with Flu along Dingle Lane on their way to the docks, he collapsed of a heart attack and died. On the 18th he was buried at Laleham. The mourners included Browning and Henry James, with wreaths from Millais and Tennyson. "From the austere tone of some of his poems" wrote Flu, "those who did not know him, could never have imagined his really bright, genial, loveable nature".

His profligate son Dick and wife Ella moved to Worcester where in 1899 their friend Elgar used Dick as his inspiration for the fifth variation of the 'Enigma Variations' – it portrays a man of frequently changing moods. Elgar was later to compose 'The Dream of Gerontius' based on the poem of John Henry Newman, the man whose style had had such an influence on Matthew Arnold.

1

Some Selected Poems

Because so few of Arnold's lyrics are popular in our own time, modern critics tend to approach them in one of three directions: as the artistic or unconscious forerunners of his later critical essays on poetry; as revelations about, or elucidators of, an unremarkable life whose emotional Everest seems to have been the love of the French (or possibly Swiss) woman Marguerite; and as an expression of his search for a balance between the strict canons of classical art and the uncontrolled idiosyncrasies of romanticism.

Thus the intrinsic qualities of Arnold's early poetry are often overlooked. And Arnold being Arnold, his poetry cannot be properly evaluated without reference to what he judged poetry to be, as famously expressed in *Essays in Criticism, Culture and Anarchy* and the 1853 preface to *Poems: A New Edition*. These critiques, as Buckler* says, and his letters to Clough provide our purest – though not necessarily most honest – sources for his poetic theory. But do they truly reflect the aims of his lyrics as written long before he came to concretise in his criticisms what he thought he was expressing – or felt he should be expressing?

Buckler, for instance, favours Arnold the model-seeker, the experimental man of masks, over Arnold the youthfully self-conscious poet agonising over his emotions. Allot favours the more traditional view of Arnold as the poet caught between his objectivity and his self-denying preferences. There is no doubt that Arnold does use personae in some of his lyrics ('The Youth of Man' for instance) as too he does in his comic Baron von Thunder-Ten-Tronkh letters, just as there is no doubt when he speaks from an uncluttered intellect

On the Poetry of Matthew Arnold: Essays in Critical Reconstruction, 1982

1

(as in 'Dover Beach'). In such an analysis there is a progression from the lack of firm stylistic or temperamental security in his earlier lyrics to the supreme self-confidence of his later ones.

Nor can we divorce Arnold's personality from his poetry. His father's repression of both his emotional and sexual outlets may have expressed itself in his austerity of style; his doubts as to his ability to express himself not only simply but succinctly may well have come from his father's criticism of – and disappointment in – his intellectual abilities.

Both English and German Romanticism were heavily influential on the young Arnold. Despite Coleridge, English Romanticism disdained self-explanation, preferring to express itself through its own artistic creations. German Romanticism pontificated upon itself at every opportunity, and its depressing influence (in the sense of an over-philosophizing and overt self-consciousness) may be seen in Byron's 'Manfred'.

Byron with his monumental life, his existential quest for his own meaning, his search for a universal morality beyond the petty prejudices he felt to characterise his own times, was the earliest influence on Arnold. But to the later Arnold, Byron was perceived as too much the Romantic poet in his 'capriciousness' – the slackness of poetic structure, the emphasis on immediate sensitoriness, and the slowness of forward movement in its concentration of detail to the detriment of the overall thrust (as illustrated by 'Don Juan'). At Oxford his influence was replaced by that of Goethe, as a German Romanticist who, to the young Arnold, embraced in his poetry the classical aesthetics of art balanced by the poet's individual voice.

After the Napoleonic invasions, Germany, as yet ununited, was trying to exert a distinctive cultural identity independent of the French culture that had dominated it for the previous hundred years. It found it by eschewing French neo-classicism in favour of an English Romanticism of self-expression and individual genius, exemplified not by Byron or Shelley but Shakespeare – indeed, to such an extent that he became the German national poet as much as the English one. But there is a basic dichotomy in German Romanticism, and it lay between its tendency to pay artistic lip-service to the classical unities and its nationalistic search for a tutelary genius, of both art and race, as perceived in Shakespeare with his "native woodnotes wild", a genius it was eventually to find in Goethe.

Broadly speaking, the aesthetics underpinning German Romanticism follow a chronological progression. Winckelmann had proposed that the best art is impersonal, expressing an ideal proportion and balance as opposed to expressing one's own individuality, as if art tended towards an ideal form. Fichte built on this, arguing that the artist creates a world in which beauty as much as truth is a moral virtue. Kant took this further. Beauty, he declared, is what satisfies a disinterested need. So a beautiful object has no function but exists purely for itself. Therefore judgements of beauty are not expressions of personal preference but are universal. To Hegel, art religion and philosophy are the bases of the highest spiritual development, so natural objects are reorganized by art to satisfy aesthetic demands: an object ugly in itself can become beautiful in and because of its aesthetic context. Schopenhauer thought these aesthetic demands were akin to the Platonic ideals or forms of the universe that exist beyond the world of experience. By contemplating them for their own sake one achieves aesthetic satisfaction by union with the eternal reality.

These views slowly move towards the concept of Art for Art's sake. Noticeably Arnold refuses to discuss the Romantic poets in his *Essays on Criticism* on the grounds that they are too recent for objective assessment. But his excuse may have masked an unwillingness to admit their profound influence on his own youthful endeavours. I suspect he also recognised that the dichotomy at the heart of German romanticism reflected his own approach to the aesthetics of poetry, that his admired French neo-classicism constrained not only the artistic freedom of the poetic tradition he was born into but also his inherent artistic rebelliousness – the Romanticism of his youthful reading. On an Oedipal level some might interpret this as the influence of the restrictive father being challenged by the burgeoning self-expressiveness of the son.

Romanticism, with its emphasis on individuality and passion for its own sake, he considered a one-sided doctrine (as he wrote to Clough in 1845) that surrendered rationality to emotion. Its counterbalance was the tendency to use art to reform or educate, to make it edifying, something equally distasteful to Arnold. "How deeply unpoetical the age and all one's surroundings are," as he famously wrote, with its disturbing and anti-Wordsworthian implication that art cannot be found (or perhaps should not be found) in the workaday world we live in.

Wordsworth was Arnold's lifelong mentor and his mother's close Westmorland neighbour. He was a poet not concerned with the effect of nature on the external senses but on what it internally released, the effect of a natural object upon the mind and how it is metamorphosed aesthetically and becomes endowed with a something beyond its own self. Andrew Keanie, in his *William Wordsworth*, illustrates this with the following quotation from *The Prelude*:

> ... An auxiliar light
> Came from my mind, which on the setting sun
> Bestowed new splendour; the melodious birds ...
> ... obeyed
> A like dominion, and the midnight storm
> Grew darker in the presence of my eye.

This highly personal, metamorphosing, experience is absent in Arnold's work, though he recognises its power. His inclination was more towards an objective Berkleyan analysis of its effect upon the mind, and what meaning – if extractable – it holds for us.

The view of Arnold as the poet of statement, the observer rather than the partaker, pays tribute to the influence of the classical poets on him. Homer with his plain language and 'grand style'; Sophocles, who placed the exploration of man's mind and his place in the world above all other poetic considerations; Pindar the lyric poet, master of choric self-abstraction, and thus nearest to Arnold's own prosodic preferences, who in his youth had lost a poetry competition because of the excessive use of ornamentation and personal attitude in his verse, impressing upon him – as it was to do on Arnold – the need to control both his use of language and the subjective desire to imprint himself on his art. And of course Vergil, for his propriety, his humanity, his sensitivity in terms of aural and structural balance.

What then is the basis of Arnold's poetics amidst this welter of influences and self-judgementalism and search for artistic identity? Perhaps we can do no more than accept at face value what he himself stated in a letter to Clough in 1853 concerning our aesthetic needs: "I am glad you like The Scholar-Gypsy – but what does it do for you? Homer animates – Shakespeare animates ... what they [mankind] want is something to animate and ennoble them – not merely to add zest to their melancholy or grace to their dreams. – I believe a feeling of this kind is the basis of my nature – and of my poetics."

'The Forsaken Merman'

This narrative poem appeared in *The Strayed Reveller and Other Poems by 'A'*, Arnold's first volume of poetry, published in 500 copies in February 1849. The 'A' was a laconic Arnold pretending to diffidence. The plot concerns a merman (the narrator) waiting on the seashore with his children for his human wife to return to him, but he waits in vain. The poem contains no universal truths or deep observations on human nature save by implication from the depicted situation. And by implication we can read into it – if you agree with Buckler – the theme of over-sophisticated man alienated from his naturalistic origins, more concerned with system than meaning. I prefer to hear in its elegiac plaint and rhythmic variation of speed the theme of lost or sundered love.

Clough suggested some minor factual errors be corrected and Byron's 'Manfred' suggested some of the imagery in lines 115-146; the source of the plot may have come from Hans Christian Andersen but otherwise the poem owes its inception to Arnold's repressed emotions, for almost certainly the sub-text is that of Arnold's hopeless love for Marguerite in the merman's plea for his Margaret to return to him. The traditional theme of the mermaid who comes from the sea to live on land is inverted, and may reflect Arnold's travelling to the foreign environment of Switzerland to meet Marguerite, who refuses to leave her homeland for him. Irreconcilable merman and human, Matthew and Marguerite, are sundered for ever.

Its appeal lies in its plain style, one of both directness and repetitiveness that seem to imitate a tidal circularity, and a rhythmic variation now echoing the slow grinding ebb of the sea (in the stanzas that refer to shore or church), now its inshore rush in the underwater stanzas, as the merman's emotions vary between despair or exhortation, pity for his children, nostalgia, and finally – as so often with Arnold – a controlled resignation.

Memorial Verses

On 23 April 1850 Wordsworth died, and at the urging of his son-in-law, Edward Quillinan, Arnold wrote *Memorial Verses*, published in 1852. This is not a personal elegy, though Arnold had known Wordsworth since his youth, nor a formal elegy in the form of a pastoral or dirge; it is more a poetic cenotaph to someone he deeply admired, and was an occasion to sum up the three distinct qualities of what Arnold considered to be the three greatest European poets of the first half of the 19th century – Byron, Goethe, and Wordsworth. Arnold was drawing away from the poetic mentor of his youth, Byron, who occupies a less exalted position than the other two poets in this poem, but Arnold recognises the energy and life of action behind his poetry, a renaissance union of artistic sensibility and heroic action that Arnold admired and recognised the lack of in himself. Goethe is seen as the wise analyst of Europe's political and cultural ills (a post Arnold himself secretly aspired to), and Wordsworth as the healer, spiritual and natural, who brought colour and insight into the stale everyday.

Quillinan described the poem as a "triple epicede" (funeral ode) and thought the poem too detached and formal. Arnold recognised its formality in a letter to Clough, describing the poem as having been written "in the grand style", and certainly it contains no personal emotion at the loss of a family friend. And like many of Arnold's melancholic poems it develops from elegy into literary criticism, from the passing of an era into a criticism of life, with typical despair for the future of cultural sensibilities:

> Time may restore us in his course
> Goethe's sage mind and Byron's force;
> But where will Europe's latter hour
> Again find Wordsworth's healing power?
> (59-62)

"Goethe" wrote Arnold in *Essays in Criticism, Second Series*, 1888, "lays his finger on [Byron's] real source of weakness both as a man and as a poet. 'The moment he reflects he is a child'." Arnold did not deny Byron's power and energy, writing of his "Titanism" in *On the Study of Celtic Literature*, 1867. Goethe opined: "I call the classic healthy, the romantic sickly". Carlyle spoke of "the diseased self-conscious state of Literature" in 1831, and both comments may have prompted Arnold's summing up of early 19th century literature as too obsessed with self-doubt and the mind's dialogue with itself to the detriment of simple objectivity, as expressed in his preface to the 1853 volume of Poetry.

The three poets are thus balanced against one another in terms of their suitability as models for the aspiring poet. Byron and Goethe are seen as too detached, godlike almost, from the problems of the times. Only Wordsworth can return poetry to its original simplicity of purpose and expression.

Switzerland (the Marguerite poems)

In September 1848 Arnold visited Thun in Switzerland, a well-known resort for the British. There, it appears, he met a girl whom he calls Marguerite, celebrated in a series of poems he later grouped together as *Switzerland*. These were written over a number of years and the grouping is not chronological: he regularly went on holiday to Switzerland and subscribed to the Alpine Club. In Thun, the French poet de Senancourt had written *Obermann* in 1804, a novel that had a great influence on Arnold as can be seen in 'Stanzas in Memory of the Author of *Obermann*' (1852) and 'Obermann Once More' (1867).

Did Arnold make up Marguerite? Was she real but fantasised about? Murray suggests she may have been an erotic extension of a French Protestant girl he had met near his family home at Fox Howe in Westmoreland. Hints of a previous secret affair in Paris in 1847, possibly based on a visit in 1846, were given by Clough in a letter written in February 1847 to Arnold's mother: "his stay … seems to have been very satisfactory to him". The girl may possibly have been the actress Elisa Rachel. Rachel was later to be commemorated in the 1863 sonnet 'Rachel', a poem of fading beauty linked to the faded love for Marguerite, of sere September, and the retreat of the mind into itself, with all its memories and experiences concentrated to a core object.

None of Arnold's biographers – as far as I am aware – submit any evidence of who Marguerite was or even if she existed. Arnold wrote to Clough on 29th September 1848 of lingering "one day at the Hotel Bellevue for the sake of the blue eyes of one of its inmates", though the sixth poem in the sequence implies that Marguerite had eyes of grey. Was this 'Daughter of France' a guest, a maid, a married woman?

1. 'Meeting, 1849' – this was composed on his second visit to Thun, but this time his will holds back his passion, "Be counsell'd and retire". The "enkerchief'd hai" looks forward to the fifth poem in the sequence ('To Marguerite – Continued') with its "enisled" and "enclasping" – the 'en' prefix suggesting imprisonment, his own imagination held back by reality, his passion by rationality.

2. 'Parting, 1849' – this rationality now becomes symbolised by the cold snowy mountains, an object to flee to from the guilt he feels for his passion for Marguerite. There is the tension between impersonal nature and his own sexual drive (at a guess he had slept with Marguerite by the time he wrote the poem). The wished flight to the mountains may symbolise the stern puritanical presence of his father and hoped-for forgiveness. There is an element of masculine sexual hypocrisy – now he has had her he can despise her for giving in to him and for her similar past with other men – others have kissed her, "others strain'd to that breast". This tension between passion and guilt, Marguerite and the mountain coolness, is resolved in the last stanza where "the stir of the forces/ Whence issued the world" refers both to the womb and natural phenomena. The metrical structure mirrors the tension, the various stanzas having numerous unrhymed lines and different metrical lengths.

3. 'A Farewell, 1849' – a clash between the force of love and its need of control ("the keen, unscrupulous course" echoing Dr Arnold's stern will), but the rarity of love makes it of more value. Arnold then attempts to moralise from this, but these stanzas really are commonplace generalisations about self-discipline hardly derived from the force of the opening stanzas, though uttered in a fresh way. Love is reduced to a platonic friendship for each of them, and I feel this is an excuse on Arnold's part: either he is feeling sexually guilty (or his sexual passion for her is dying – "this heart … to be long loved was never framed"), and so he attempts to console Marguerite and compromise with his guilt by proposing an asexual world, or else she is falling out of love with him for his lack of resoluteness,

and to save his self-esteem he tries to prove they really are soul-mates.

4. 'Isolation. To Marguerite, 1849' – "Thou lov'st no more" is the theme, with Arnold's falling back on the strength of his own loneliness. A classical (and Keatsian) reference intrudes somewhat irrelevantly with the story of Endymion and Luna.

5. 'To Marguerite – Continued, 1852' – The theme is now one of separation, mental and geographic ("The unplumb'd salt, estranging sea"), that has the added resonance of Arnold's partiality that England should be more a part of Europe than of the world. The end of the love-affair has been reached.

The poem's imagery has similarities to that of 'Dover Beach' written (though not completed) shortly afterwards, not only in the line quoted above but in the sea imagery of the first verse that is figurative of Arnold's sense of hopelessness, not just for the future of their love but for his inability to deal in general with life's vicissitudes:

> Yes! in the sea of life enisled,
> With echoing straits between us thrown,
> Dotting the shoreless watery wild,
> We mortal millions live alone.
>
> (1-4)

Arnold added three more poems, though one – 'A Dream', a fine poem on the desirable's rushing past our grasp – was later dropped from the sequence possibly due to its expansion of a momentary experience into a universal metaphor for the life of man. As such it is tonally at odds with the rest of the sequence.

6. 'Absence', 1852 – his love for Marguerite is not forgotten and he sees her image in the "fair stranger's eyes of grey" of Frances Wightman whom he married in 1851. The core of the poem is that rationality cannot erase memories of passion, and yet is that rationality really to be desired – "stay with me Marguerite, still"!?

7. 'The Terrace at Berne', written, as he points out, ten years later. This is Arnold looking back objectively on the affair, the realisation that their love was a fleeting passion, that they are forever apart ("meets and quits again"), which is summed up and finalised in the last stanza: "And Marguerite I shall see no more". Love, and the cold mountains, are relegated to the past. The simple rhyming pattern of A, B, A, B well compliments love's ascent to oblivion.

In 1855 Tennyson's *Maud: A Monodrama* had appeared: a youth's powerful mental conflict between persisting in his seemingly hopeless love and leaving it for a new future. Arnold may have been influenced by it when he grouped his poems in a sequence – thus 'A Memory Picture' being excluded because it is a recollection as opposed to a start to a doomed affair; 'A Dream' was too allegorical to include, even though framed as a dream, the darting river of life they are sailing along being relevant to no love object but to life in general. Even so, the sequence has too little conflict – as it begins the poet seems half determined on its demise; there is little passion and none of Maud's characterisations. Arnold would have done better to have unzipped the sequence and released the poems as stand-alone plaints. That said, they have a refreshing individuality in their emotional imagery and approach to the problems of love that smacks more of experience – or at least genuineness – than does the more controlled sequence of 'Faded Leaves', inspired by his future wife Fanny Wightman.

'Tristram and Iseult'

This transition from love of Marguerite to love of Fanny is probably the sub-text of 'Tristram and Iseult' (1852), Tristram losing Iseult of Cornwall and marrying Iseult of Brittany (according to the legends only because of the name). The selection of two Iseults – one name, two women – seems to imply a division of Arnold's love between Marguerite and Fanny.

Arnold had first read the love-story in Thun, and the memory of his lost love for Marguerite must still have been active. This chronicling of a lost love is accompanied by Arnold's awareness of the loss of youth, like his love being now no more than "shadow and dream". The setting is Brittany where the dying Tristram, somewhat cruelly, has sent to Cornwall for his real love Iseult the Fair to come and heal him. Various characters (and various prosodies and rhyme schemes as well as different forms) tell or comment on the action; but there is little action and no central core to the poem that the characters can centre on. No form or rhyme scheme is made personal to the different characters, and in terms of characterisation it is difficult to tell the two Iseults apart. As in many of Arnold's attempts at dramatic poetry the reader is not only left waiting for something to happen but feels the characters are too.

'Lines Written in Kensington Gardens'

This 1852 poem, consciously influenced by Wordsworth's sonnet 'Composed upon Westminster Bridge, Sept. 3, 1802', depicts the assertion of nature in the heart of a great city. But it differs from Wordsworth's vision in that it gives an anthropomorphic expression to this nature, a beating heart amidst the mechanism of its man-made - and thus literally artificial – surroundings. The rural Pan abstracts the narrator from the huge world, which roars hard by and becomes the gardens if only for a brief moment – an anthropomorphism hinted at not only at the start of the poem with its red-boled pine-trees sacred to Pan, but more explicitly so in the references to elms and chestnuts (deleted after the first edition) that were also sacred to the god. These arboreal associations remind us that Arnold was a keen student of both botany and its traditional lore, a scholarship made poetically overt in 'Thyrsis'. And as in 'Thyrsis' we are also reminded of one of the great Arnoldian themes:

> I, on men's impious uproar hurl'd,
> Think often, as I hear them rave,
> That peace has left the upper world
> And now keeps only in the grave.
> (25-8)

'The Youth of Nature'

"Finished Wordsworth; pindaric" says his diary for the 4th of June 1852. This pindaric is 'The Youth of Nature', which recalls a visit Arnold made to The Lakes a few weeks after the death of Wordsworth in 1850. The Pindaric ode is marked by lack of rhyme and irregular line length, interrupted train of thought, and "torrential" energy as

Horace described it. 'The Youth of Nature' certainly moves quickly, and though marked by typically Arnoldian restraint contains a welter of sense-impressions. The poem asks whether nature's beauty is intrinsic or existing only in the poet's eye. Is our view of Windermere a sense impression or has Wordsworth created a new reality of it for us? Nature's response is that "The poet who sings them may die/ But they are immortal and live." The poem shows a number of themes in which Arnold was interested:

Pastoral elegy:

> Nature is fresh as of old
> Is lovely; a mortal is dead.
>> (11-12)

> Race after race, Man after man ...
> – They are dust, they are changed, they are gone!
> I remain.
>> (129-134)

Parnassus and materialism:

> He grew old in an age he condemn'd
> He look'd on the rushing decay
> Of the times which had sheltered his youth
> And like the Theban seer,
> Died in his enemies' day ...
>> (28-35)

> Thebes was behind him in flames ...
> Nor did reviving Thebes
> See such a prophet again.
>> (41-47)

Tiresias the blind androgynous seer hints at Sophocles here, Arnold's favourite classical author. As in Empedocles we recognise in Tiresias the alienated figure with whom Arnold empathised.

Berkeleyan philosophy:

> ... is it you [Nature] ...
> ... that fill us with joy,
> Or the poet who sings you so well?
>> (59-62)

– lines that refer us to Berkeley's claim that God (or nature in Arnold) not only is sufficient cause of our ideas but is also what keeps things in being when they were not present in the field of any human perception. Wordsworth may have revealed the inner spirit of nature more than any other philosopher or poet, but the Berkeleyan belief (later to find its apotheosis in 'Thyrsis') is reaffirmed:

> Like stars in the deep of the sky ...
> But are lost when their watcher is gone.
> (72-74)

'The Youth of Man'

Later in 1852 Arnold completed a companion piece, 'The Youth of Man'. Here the 29 year old Arnold – taking different standpoints – looks ahead to the approach of middle-age. Its opening lines carry over the resolution of the 'Youth of Nature':

> We, O Nature, depart,
> Thou survivest us!

Again, we have reference to Berkeleyan philosophy, i.e. that if God gave minds the monopoly of causal activity then it is our minds that give shape to external reality:

> Nature is nothing; her charm
> Lives in our eyes which can paint,
> Lives in our hearts which can feel.
> (36-38)

But age brings the realisation that youth feels itself alive through an empathy with nature and its life-force, and once we suspect that that admiration is fading with age, leaving us to grow old in darkness and pain (58), then with failure to experience the spirit of nature comes failure to feel oneself to be a living part of it. And to the 29 year old Arnold the oneness with the "Murmur of living" (51) seems to be fragmenting as his youth fades.

There are stylistic hints of Shelley ("I die! I faint! I fail!") a triad of phrases progressing (or in Shelley regressing) to a desired result:

Murmur of living,
Stir of existence,
Soul of the world!
    (51-3)

as can also be seen in 'Thyrsis' where a generalisation concentrates into a particular object: "I knew each field, each flower, each stick" (32). The influence of Wordsworth's 'Intimations of Immortality' is also very much in evidence:

... they gaze –
Airs from the Eden of youth
Awake and stir in their soul;
The past returns – they feel
What they are, alas! What they were.
    (90-4)

'Requiescat'

This is a four-stanza poem published in 1853, each stanza of four lines having Arnold's favourite lyric rhyme-scheme A, B, A, B. The question is, who was the subject and what did she mean to Arnold? – or, if she was imaginary, does the poem imply that Arnold was about to say goodbye to a part of his life that was increasingly enervating him?

The most obvious choice is Marguerite, the subject of the 'Switzerland' sequence, though this argument is based on using as evidence lack of evidence to the contrary. Whoever Marguerite was, there is no other reference to her, inside or outside Arnold's works; and the nominal subject of 'Requiescat', from the poem's purposefully opaque hints, was obviously someone in the public eye:

Her mirth the world required;
    She bathed it in smiles of glee.
    (5-6)

But here also is a woman whose public persona is at odds with her private yearnings:

But her heart was tired, tired,
And now they let her be.
(7-8)

This surely cannot be Marguerite, that figure in the shadows. Was it then perhaps the Swiss actress Elisa Rachel? Better known she certainly was, but she lived until at least 1863 when Arnold was composing the Rachel sonnets. Was she someone Arnold did not know except by reputation?

The dichotomies of her life are expressed through a number of verbal juxtapositions – "roses/yew", "cabin'd/ample" and so on, reflecting the clash between her public persona and her private needs. This dichotomy is expressed structurally in each stanza, where the first two lines deal with her public exuberance and the last two lines with her inner weariness, the hectic mask against the private peace. This duality is tracked by the overall movement of the lyric from public mirth to public cenotaph, from private peace to private grave, becoming one in "the vasty hall of death", both monumental tomb and encrypted coffin.

Arnold obviously had empathy for this constant predicament in her life, and this empathy expresses itself in the narrator's rhetorical exclamation of "Ah, would that I did too!" (4). Save for this line – if we take it at its face value – there is no pang of grief, no new rhythm or emotional upsurge to express personal loss, and my own view is that the heroine is the imaginary embodiment of Arnold's awareness of his own temperamental contradictions. And as a figurative vehicle for these contradictions – sensitive melancholic poet against the dinner-party lioniser of laconic wit, the pretended outrager of social conventions who quietly wished to live in a nobler and surer world – does it carry the sub-text of marking his decision to abandon poetry for prose? Arnold, like the heroine, was tired of being in the public eye – by this time three editions of his poetry had already ensured his reputation.

The third stanza is redundant in that it adds little to the subject-matter of the poem or furtherance of her personality (indeed it needs no furtherance as the emphasis is simply and purely on her public versus private side), and is repetitive of stanza 2. This repetition may be conscious in that it reinforces the theme.

Maybe some things are best left a mystery, for whatever the facts behind the poem, its lyrical yet dramatic simplicity, its growing generalisation from self to universality, have ensured its popularity to the present day.

'Growing Old'

This poem, published in 1867, rejects the ideal view of old age ("'Tis not to have our life/ Mellow'd and soften'd"), and concentrates on the physical and intellectual deterioration of ageing ("And not once feel that we were ever young"), until the final irony of hearing (but not being aware of?) a hypocritical world "applaud the hollow ghost/ Which blamed the living man."

"Grow old along with me/ The best is yet to be!" starts Browning's 'Rabbi Ben Ezra', as if with ideal optimism, but the best to Browning was the self-doubt that age brings, the coming to terms with one's imperfections, the reconciliation with God in life's completion of youth with age in death. But God is missing from Arnold's poem, as is his normal detachment: instead we are left with a controlled despair. Where Arnold's lyric looks out to the world and sees an uncaring, unresponsive reality, Browning's ode looks inward to wrestle from the narrator's mind the consolation of a divine answer. Both poems start from different viewpoints and opposing voices, but interestingly neither makes an appeal to the old common faith in God, each poet having to find his own answer to replace what once was a commonplace belief.

'The Last Word'

The bitterness of 'Growing Old' turns into contempt in 'The Last Word' for those who submit to age's appeasement with controversy, then becomes a call for action. The lyric comprises four stanzas, rhyming A, A, B, B split into two sections. The first two stanzas are sardonically contemptuous – no point in contending, the narrator says, so why not die quietly in bed? The second two stanzas switch to exhortation: better men than you have suffered the same despair; fight one last time and die in battle. No creeping into a narrow bed – the conventional way of dying – but openly meeting death in war. Here is Arnold's failure in life and art, here is his thwarted ambition – to combine artistic sensibility with heroic achievement, to emulate, we may say, Ben Jonson's challenging of a Spaniard to single combat on a Flemish battlefield in 1597, killing him and Homerically stripping him of his armour. But the times were too Victorian for such ethical singularity, and side by side with Arnold's hero-archetype went the ever-present mentor urging him to uniformity in art, life and politics. But then which of us has not fantasised and fought our way through to the riches of King Solomon's mines, only to creep into work next day?

There are obvious similarities to Byron's 'On This Day I Complete My Thirty-Sixth Year'. Byron's theme is that of the heroic leap of resolution, from youthful self-obsessed passion to the equally passionate, yet paradoxically rational, self-sacrifice of middle-age:

> If thou regret'st thy youth, why live?
>
> ... A soldier's grave for thee the best;
> Then look around, and choose thy ground,
>   And take thy rest.
>   (33-40)

The same theme of life's asserting itself in its own death is seen in Dylan Thomas' 'Do Not Go Gentle Into That Good Night', suggesting that Arnold's poem has had an influence on the theme if not the structure of Thomas' poem:

> Though wise men at their end know dark is right,
> Because their words had forked no lightning they
> Do not go gentle into that good night. (DNGGITGN 4-6)
> Better men fared thus before thee;
> Fired their ringing shot and pass'd,
> Hotly charged – and sank at last.
>   ('The Last Word' 10-12)

The differences between the two poems lie in tone and structure, Thomas' poem – though lacking the introductory sardonicism and its balancing call to arms of 'The Last Word' – being controlled by the upsurge of a single sustained emotion, where Arnold's is a philosophical, albeit ironic, exhortation to conquer criticism with heroism.

'Palladium'

This 1867 lyric poem of 24 lines, sonnet-like with its final two-line explication of the theme, directly compares the soul to the Palladium at Troy, beneath which Hector and Helen and Ajax play out the war of life. Again, we are reminded of Arnold's claim that the highest art is a combination of sensibility and heroic challenge, and of his predilection for clothing aesthetic questions in the armour of war.

The Palladium refers to a wooden image of Pallas Athene, goddess of wisdom and the civilised arts, that was taken to Troy where Helenus prophesied that while it stood Troy could not fall; unfortunately the wily Odysseus stole it. The Romans claimed he only stole a copy and that Aeneas rescued the real one and took it to Rome where the Vestal Virgins took charge of it. By analogy, if the Palladium is stolen, man's soul is stolen, and Arnold means here both the inheriting by Rome of classical civilisation and the seduction of modern intellect by materialism and Romantic 'caprice' – over-individuality in life-style, art and society. As may be seen in much of his poetry, one of his strengths lay in excising his emotion from his melancholy, a calm objectivity that others would say was his poetic downfall.

By intellect, he meant the application of the formality and objectivity that was seen as the hallmark of Classicism. At this time Parnassianism was all the rage in France, an artistic movement named after Mt. Parnassos which is directly equated with the Palladium in the lines:

> Mountains surround it, and sweet virgin air;
> Cold plashing, past it, crystal waters roll;
>
> (10-11)

the "virgin air" linking Parnassus to the virgin Athene and her Palladium. It was a movement that Arnold the Francophile took fully on board.

'Obermann Once More'

This was started in 1865 when Arnold was abroad as Foreign Assistant Commissioner of Schools and published in the 1867 volume. Written in the familiar four-line A, B, A, B stanza, its theme is that of dying spiritually and the need, perhaps cyclical, for self-renewal in both the individual and society. It follows the structure of 'Stanzas in Memory of the author of *Obermann*', the inspiration coming from the natural scenery of Glion; but in the later poem change is seen in this scenery:

> But now the old is out of date,
> The new is not yet born.
> And who can be alone elate,
> While the world lies forlorn?
> (245-248)

Notice the Tennysonian use of assonance and alliteration here. Tennyson's influence – from the youthful if unacknowledged reading of his poetry by Arnold – is also apparent in the rhythm and structure of lines 129-132

> She broke her flutes, she stopp'd her sports,
> Her artists could not please;
> She tore her books, she shut her courts,
> She fled her palaces.

where its speed of syntactical abbreviation reminds us of 'The Lady of Shalott' of 1844. But there is none of that poem's resignation at an unfruitful death: in Arnold's poem the spirit of Obermann urges him to inspire "Hope to a World New-Made", then fades and leaves the poet gazing across the Swiss lakes into an optimistic future, "where I saw the morning break". Rare in Arnold, we have here the triumph of hope over actuality.

'Dover Beach'

Written on his honeymoon at Dover in 1851, though not published until 1867, 'Dover Beach' appears to have undergone a number of revisions, not least under the influence (in the last stanza) of Darwinism, where the poem resignedly bows to evolutionary theory. It comprises four stanzas or verse-paragraphs, of irregular rhyme and scansion, that mirror the fragmentation of faith and by implication, for all Arnold's counterpleading, the inevitable cooling of his and Fanny's love.

Sources include Thucydides, Newman, Carlyle and Milton. Its formal stately style is seen in the use of the Miltonic latinate construction of adjective-noun-adjective, as in "tremulous cadence slow" (13) and "vast edges drear" (27) which empower by contrast the monosyllabic keywords – from "calm" "full" and "fair" at the start to "struggle" "flight" and "night" at the end – that carry the poem forward to its conclusion. According to S.P. Sen Gupta the inspiration for:

> And we are here as on a darkling plain
> Swept with confused alarms of struggle and flight,
> Where ignorant armies clash by night
>
> (35-7)

is derived jointly from Thucydides' description in his *History of the Peloponnesian War* of the Battle of Epipolae in 413 BC and Newman's sermon of 1839 (which itself may have been inspired by Thucydides): "Controversy, at least in this age, ... is a sort of night-battle, where each fights for himself, and friend and foe stand together." Carlyle noted in *Characteristics* how "in these new days [1831] ... Not Godhead, but an iron, ignoble circle of Necessity embraces all things", marvellously expressed by Arnold in "the grating roar/ Of pebbles", and "the vast edges drear/ And naked shingles of the world".

This is geological imagery applied to a poetic theme. In fact, with the large amount of geological references, stark, concrete and austere, we might even say this is poetry applied to a geological theme. Hutton's theory – that the geological environment has changed and continues to change at a constant rate – caused a universal furore from 1833 onwards to which Arnold was not immune. Just as there is no certitude even in the rocks on which we live (the terror of an earthquake is that our psychological certainties are upheaved as well), so is there no certitude in the faiths by which we live, and for the narrator the truth that sustains love is all that is left to us in the face of such nihilism.

For 'Dover Beach' is both a love-lyric and a meditation on the decay of faith, the poem's melancholy being quietly sustained by a philosophical objectivity rather than by any emotional upsurge, a restrained and formal observation of the ebbing of once firm beliefs.

This is a theme also found in 'Stanzas from the Grande Chartreuse'. The two themes are combined in the last stanza where Arnold – searching for anchorage amidst change and decay – asks for the refuge of truth to be his and Fanny's mainstay against the collapse of faith (the land of dreams) and the violent selfishness of human nature.

But this desperate appeal to Fanny, and the poem's use of imagery similar to that of 'To Marguerite – Continued' of 1852 in the 'Switzerland' sequence:

> A God, a God their severance ruled!
> And bade betwixt their shores to be
> The unplumb'd, salt, estranging sea.
>   (22-24)

hint guiltily that in a godless 'Dover Beach' Fanny is no more than a substitute Marguerite.

The sheer simplicity and hard vividness of the descriptions, combining with its uneven rhythms to generate of themselves the theme, have rightly made this poem a perennial favourite. And of course there is that perennial hope that, being sapient, we may in time find an answer to the uncertainties of evolution itself.

2

Arnold and the Epic Simile
'The Scholar-Gypsy'
'Sohrab and Rustum'
'Balder Dead'

Arnold attempted to embody what he saw as the beauties of Homeric epic in two epyllia (short epics like "Paradise Regained'), though neither used a Greek theme: 'Sohrab and Rustum' (a Persian theme) in 1853, and 'Balder Dead' (a Norse theme) in 1855, described by Clough as "A Scandinavian Apollo ... in blank verse, in the neo-Homeric manner." Whereas 'Merope' (1857) stylistically imitates Sophocles the two earlier poems eschew dramatic structure in favour of epic qualities:

- aristocratic formalism
- single combat
- tribal conflict
- superhuman heroes
- stately speeches
- crowd scenes
- elaborate ('Homeric') similes.

But Arnold's style is plainer and more direct than Homer's (qualities he admired, yet Homer is often difficult and obscure in his use of language). For instance Arnold frequently uses the paratactic "and", an ancient stylistic device of piling and juxtaposing images or events rapidly, in clausal form with no or minimal links between them, familiar to us from the bible: in Rustum's lament, lines 795-826, *And* begins the line 17 times, including five lines that begin with it consecutively. Also, he is more concerned with the unproductive death of the hero than with Homer's emphasis upon the supreme act of bravery for the tribe – Arnold's heroes are existentialist, Homer's are unquestioning actors for the tribal mind-set.

Several adaptations of both Homer's and Vergil's epics are incorporated in 'Sohrab and Rustum' and 'Balder Dead' (the reader will find them listed in Highet's *The Classical Tradition*, Oxford, repr. 1967), from repeated conventions to scenic framing. With respect to the similes these are mostly drawn from nature, yet Arnold makes them appropriate to their oriental or northern settings. They are often typically Arnoldian in their controlled underlay of grief or melancholy. He is of course much influenced by the classical (or Homeric) use of simile, but Milton's extension of its possibilities and Arnold's own quirkiness of use are very much factors to be taken into consideration.

The Homeric simile

As Arnold said of Milton's grand style, great poetic imagery shows itself in a "pregnant allusive way". "Pregnant" reminds us that classical poets used the simile as literary sympathetic magic: just as the farmer and his wife copulated in a ploughed field to induce a fertile crop by the magic of sympathetic action, so the ancient poets used the simile to induce life and fecundity into the plot. Childless couples in Dorset (and others) still copulate on the genitals of the Cerne Abbas giant, as Dylan Thomas appreciated when he wrote 'In the White Giant's Thigh'.

On a more practical level, the Homeric simile is characterised by three functions: relief (from the fury of action), ecphrasis (for use as pure decoration), and analogy (Homer drew his similes from humble life and the animal world, often using natural imagery as a comment on the present action or for psychological elucidation). Ecphrasis is the commonest characteristic of these similes, especially in late classical times. In Homer, and to a lesser extent Vergil, similes that acted as relief from the weariness of battle often referred to the past life of someone, to the peaceful world of home (a pathetic fallacy to escape the terror of imminent death). Both Homer and Vergil use the resonance of mythic association, but their similes are not complex and certainly not strictly analogous. For example, in *The Odyssey* where Penelope speaks of her dejection and need to choose a suitor:

You know how... the brown nightingale, perched in the dense foliage of the trees, makes her sweet music when the spring is young, and with how many turns and trills she pours out her full-throated song in sorrow for Itylus her beloved son ... whom ... she killed with her own hand. So does my inclination waver, first to this side, then to that.
(Bk XIX, 518-523, trans. E Rieu, Homer – *The Odyssey*, Penguin, 1946)

The care and indecisiveness is apparent, but where is the relevance of Itylus to her son Telemachus? Similarly in *The Aeneid* (trans. D. West, Virgil – *The Aeneid*, Penguin, 1991):

His thoughts moved swiftly, now here, now there, darting in every possible direction ... like light flickering from water in bronze vessels as it is reflected from the sun ... now flying far and wide ... rising to strike the high coffers of a ceiling.
(VIII, 20-25)

Contrary to what we expect from "strike the high coffers", Aeneas does not reach a decision.

The Miltonic simile

Both Spenser and Shakespeare used ecphrasis, but sometimes their similes look forward to future actions, an analogy of a present event to a similar one in the future. This characteristic is known as prolepsis, and its great exponent was Milton.* In *Paradise Lost* he not only refreshed the Homeric simile but made the fullest use of the ironic potential now offered by prolepsis. His similes do not come at the climax of an episode, as in Statius for example, but are homologous (simultaneous with the action), more strictly related to the episode. Analogous and proleptic in terms of both plot and character, in *Paradise Lost* they display the irony of timely existence against the backdrop of God the All-time.

Satan, squat like a toad, close at the ear of Eve, is suddenly jabbed by Ithuriel's spear and leaps up:

*I am indebted to the unpublished lecture notes of Dr Ian Fletcher for this analysis of Milton's use of prolepsis.

Discovered and surprised. As, when a spark
Lights on a heap of nitrous powder, laid
Fit for the tun, some magazine to store
Against a rumoured war the smutty grain
With sudden blaze diffused, inflames the air;
So started up, in his own shape the Fiend.
                                        (IV, 813-819)

Satan is the explosive set off by Ithuriel's spear. This also implies
that Satan is the pernicious inventor of gun-powder. Most similes in
Milton have a point-to-point application to the action, and in this
example, gun-powder looks back to the war in heaven (or forward, if
we do not know the poem), and of course it looks forward to Milton's
own time of civil war, where one artillery piece could demolish a
castle. We may illustrate this construction by use of tenor (the action
referred to) and analogue (the simile or 'likeness' sprung from it):

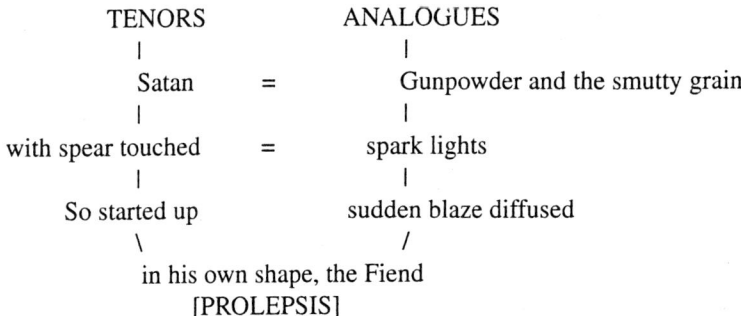

                TENORS   ANALOGUES
                   | |
                Satan   =   Gunpowder and the smutty grain
                   | |
        with spear touched   =   spark lights
                   | |
            So started up   sudden blaze diffused
                    \   /
                 in his own shape, the Fiend
                        [PROLEPSIS]

(the prolepsis is the looking forward to the war in heaven and snake
of paradisial betrayal, Satan's 'own shape' containing its past and
future manifestations).

The Arnoldian simile: 'The Scholar-Gypsy'

In *On Translating Homer* (1861-2) Arnold wrote: "Milton charges
himself so full with thought, imagination, knowledge, that his style
will hardly contain them. He is too full-stored to show us in much
detail one conception, one piece of knowledge; he just shows it to us
in a pregnant allusive way, and then he presses on to another." In his
Mixed Essays of 1877 Arnold described Milton as "our great artist
in style, our one first-rate master in the grand style." Heroic simile

being one of the elements of the grand style, how does Arnold make use of or add to its possibilities?

"Do you remember a poem of mine called 'The Scholar-Gypsy'? It was meant to fix the remembrance of those delightful wanderings of ours in the Cumner Hills before they were quite effaced", wrote Matthew in a letter to his brother Tom in May 1857. The longing for times past is apparent. There are two strands running through the poem, published in 1853, which give it this elegiac tone:

- the pastoral element of the Berkshire countryside
- the 17th century pilgrimage of the Oxford scholar in search of knowledge.

Nature and self-knowledge are woven together to express both themselves and their inter-dependence. The scholar is looking for 'truth', and Arnold associates it with the eternal cycle of nature and its reassurance. But both nature and the 17th century sense of oneness with the natural order have been overthrown by the modern age of industrialisation and its train of despair and cynicism. Arnold recognises that the past cannot be relived and the long final simile reinforces this by its reference to flight and solitude, seemingly isolated from the Victorian revolution.

Originally Arnold wished to entitle the poem 'The Wandering Mesmerist' after an interest the Arnolds had taken in hypnotism in 1844, but this smacked of delusion if not charlatanism. Arnold laments not only the loss of youth's questing energy but of the vigour of a former time; Victorian Britain, he felt, was losing its intellectual vigour and starting to atrophy. 'The Scholar-Gypsy' represented an ideal way of life no longer possible in Arnold's time, thus the framing of the plot in the pastoral form, the harking back to Arcadia, where man is at one with himself and nature, a fully rounded being fit to search for poetic truth.

The story of the Scholar-Gypsy, quoted by Arnold in his note to the poem, comes from Joseph Glanvill's *Vanity of Human Dogmatising* of 1661 which Arnold had read in 1844. It tells how a poor university scholar abandoned his studies to live with gypsies and study their traditional lore, intending to reveal their 'mystery' to the world. Dr Arnold had become Regius Professor of History at

Oxford in 1841 and we may speculate that it was his influence that got Matthew interested in local history. In lines 124-130 for instance, the winter view of Oxford from Cumnor, we glimpse the escape of the Empress Maud from the besieged city in December 1142. Camouflaged in a white cloak and with four knights she crossed the frozen Thames, glancing back at King Stephen's troops as she made her way to Abingdon. Arnold's exhortation to the scholar to flee our feverish contact and this strange disease of modern life looks back to this romantic past and forward to the theme of 'Thyrsis' whose stanzaic form it foreshadows.

The simile that terminates the poem is well signalled in true Homeric style: "As some grave Tyrian trader ...", but how effective is this simile? Like the pseudo-simile at the end of 'Sohrab and Rustum' it is extended in length (two stanzas out of the poem's 25), it is a vivid analogue of the preceding themes and, not least, an imaginative leap from the threatening world of industrialisation to the threatened world of classicism.

The simile leaves the natural and everyday imagery of the poem's philosophy and takes the reader to a single point which paradoxically is both the summation of the theme and its dissolution, where the image no longer sustains itself but leaves us contemplating a world of imaginative possibilities – a pregnant allusiveness. As such the simile lives up to Arnold's own definition of what should be its stylistic effects.

But there are distinct problems with this simile. Its very length (20 lines) puts a strain on the reader when trying to relate, and hold in the mind, tenor to analogue:

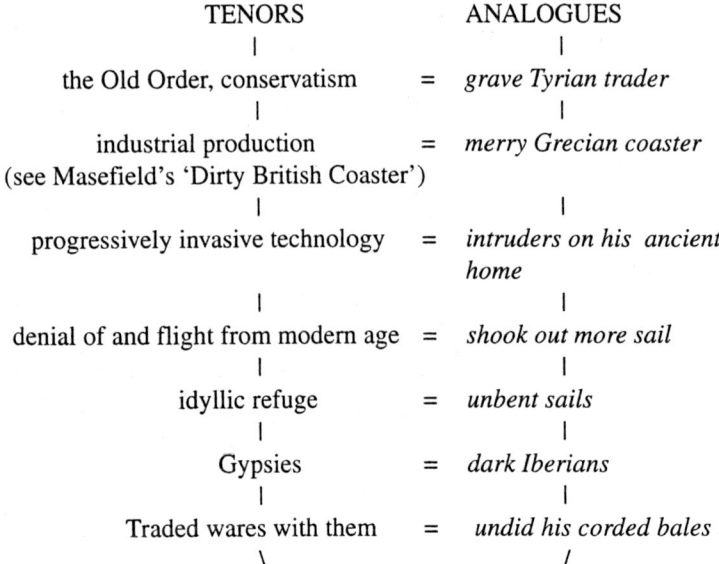

TENORS		ANALOGUES
|		|
the Old Order, conservatism	=	*grave Tyrian trader*
|		|
industrial production	=	*merry Grecian coaster*
(see Masefield's 'Dirty British Coaster')		
|		|
progressively invasive technology	=	*intruders on his ancient home*
|		|
denial of and flight from modern age	=	*shook out more sail*
|		|
idyllic refuge	=	*unbent sails*
|		|
Gypsies	=	*dark Iberians*
|		|
Traded wares with them	=	*undid his corded bales*
\		/

PROLEPSIS
(inferred – the Greek/philistine will displace the Tyrian/classicist)

This strain of holding and interpreting the tenor of the simile hides other problems:

- The Tyrians (Phoenicans) are made the heroes and the Greeks the villains, going against the prevailing attitude of the day. Although the early Victorians admired the Phoenicians for introducing technology and the alphabet to the Greeks, their overall view was that the Greeks were bringers of enlightenment and the Phoenicians oriental despots;
- The Tyrian is described in Parnassian terms, forsaking a material present for a more spiritual and formalised past of classicism; but the commonly accepted symbol of that classicism, the exploratory Greek, is what the Tyrian is fleeing from;
- The "corded bales" imply the scholar has something to trade in return for wisdom, but this is not what we infer from the poem, a receptivity by the scholar and a freely giving by the gypsies;

- Of what relevance is the past of the eastern Mediterranean "Among the Aegaean" isles to the modern Cotswolds? The "amber grapes" and "Chian wine" may represent the industrial produce of their time, but their southernness, naturalness, and attractiveness of imagery militate against the tenor of intrusive industrialisation. This problem of the relationship of modern Britain to the ancient world was to be resolved in 'Thyrsis'.

Bearing these conflicts in mind we can say that overall the simile encapsulates the theme of intellect buffeted by – and to be smothered by – the sterility of materialism. Historically where the Phoenicians went the Greeks were bound to follow, so the Tyrian/Scholar's escape would be temporary at best. In fact the Greeks were to drive the Phoenicians from trading in the north Mediterranean altogether. Prolepsis plays no part in the Homeric simile, but Milton's revolutionary use of it has moulded Arnold's use – and our expectations – of it and enables the modern reader to foresee here the triumph of industrial materialism and the retreat of spirituality, albeit paradoxically.

The syntax is occasionally incoherent: for example, the length of the simile and the movement of the action would be better served by the use of the present participle instead of the aorist tense in the cases of "descried" and "unbent". These two verbs begin and end the simile's movement, linked by a series of and + verb constructions: "Descried ... And saw ... And knew ..." "And snatch'd ... and shook ... and ... held ... and unbent sails" – a paratactic device that gives an excellent impression of hurrying to escape.

'Sohrab and Rustum'

"Milton is sufficiently great a master to imitate" Arnold wrote to John Coleridge, anent 'Sohrab and Rustum'. Clough thought it too Tennysonian, but Arnold asked him to contrast it with 'Morte D'Arthur', claiming that his own poem differed in "the issue of the style ... and in its movement". The ultimate source of the story is Sir John Malcolm's *History of Persia* (1815): Rustum, one of the leaders of the Persian army, does single combat with Sohrab, a hero of the Tartar army, near the Oxus, and having mortally wounded him discovers too late that he is his only son. A sub-text may be Arnold's deep sense of having been intellectually crushed by his father.

The poem was highly topical and its location romantically exotic. Central Asia was becoming increasingly important in British imperial affairs ever since Napoleon and Tsar Alexander had secretly met at Tilsit in 1807 (on a barge to prevent spies overhearing) to discuss a twofold attack on British India. Within days the British knew exactly what had been discussed, thanks to a foreign correspondent for *The Times* who had swum out to the barge and eavesdropped from its rafters. In 1832, Alexander Burnes, an Indian Army officer, was sent on a surveying and spying expedition to Afghanistan and Bukhara to determine what route a Russian army would take if it tried to invade India, and he published an account of his journey in 1834, *Travels into Bokhara*. It was to influence both the 'The Sick King in Bokhara' and 'The Strayed Reveller' of 1849. In 1840 a Russian army had almost frozen to death in the winter sands of the Kara Kum desert trying to take the oasis city of Khiva before the British got there. In 1842 the emir of Bukhara, a feudal tyrant caught in an ever-tightening crush between the expanding Russian empire and British India, had sided with the Russians by executing captains Conolly and Stoddart after a British army had been completely wiped out by the Afghans earlier that year in the Khyber Pass (save for one man, whom they allowed to carry the terrible news to Jalalabad), thus momentarily releasing the pressure on his emirate. A certain Reverend Wolff from Richmond bravely went to Bukhara to ascertain the truth. Whilst there he tried to convert the emir, who was about take immense delight in torturing him to a slow death when he heard that the British had again invaded Afghanistan, this time exacting revenge. Wolff was sent home loaded with gifts for "the great queen". He published an account of his travels in 1845. In 1843, the consul in Baghdad was another soldier, Major Henry Rawlinson, who had dangled upside down over the cliffs of Behistan in Persia to copy their cuneiform inscriptions, publishing his translations of them between 1846-1849, thus opening up the literature of Sumer, Akkad and Assyria to the world. The secret war of the 'Great Game' had started, and within two years of the publication of 'Sohrab and Rustum' real war would break out between Britain and Russia. Arnold's brother William had joined the Bengal Army in 1849, and continued his father's puritan crusade by writing a novel that castigated the loose sexual morals of British army officers and their wives. In 1859, FitzGerald published *The Rubaiyat of Omar Khayyam*, ostensibly based on the works of an 11th century Persian poet. In 1876 Captain Burnaby of the Horse Guards made his mad ride across the Siberian and Uzbek wastes to Khiva, he too publishing his exploits (he was to die fighting the Mahdi in the battle of Abu Klea, Sudan, in 1885). It was all stirring stuff, and this love-affair with British involvement in Central Asia persisted in English literature through Kipling (*The Man Who Would Be King*, *Stalky & Co.*, *Kim*), and innumerable Boy's Own Paper novelists who let loose the public school ethos upon the world, until the signing of the Entente Cordiale in 1904 united the two empires against that of Germany.

The poem is also consciously Homeric in its blank verse and epic style, beginning and ending with the image of the River Oxus (the modern Syr Darya in Turkmenistan). Rivers to Arnold often symbolise the elusive harmony of this world, though in this poem the Oxus also carries the rhetorical trope of symbolising the inexorable flow of earthly life. The style is plain and there are many Homeric repetitions.

As 'Sohrab and Rustum' is an epyllion or little epic, Arnold may have expected the reader to appreciate the use not only of many more similes than in 'The Scholar-Gypsy' as part of its form, but similes that fulfil the demands of ecphrasis over those of analogy and prolepsis. Though having features of the epic, the epyllion is also concerned with digressive natural description, a bringing of poetry into fresh touch with everyday objects, and a turning away from art to ritual and myth, or even primitivism. In this respect it is close to the form of the Theocritan idyll.

I have counted 21 similes in the poem, comprising 120 lines out of 874 – more than 1 in 8 – excluding the last 18 lines which are dealt with below. Of these, 10 similes comprise a simple simile of one analogue only, i.e. a single comparison is made, usually of 4 lines or less, as for example in lines 616-618 where Rustum's soul grieved:

> … as the vast tide
> Of the bright rocking Ocean sets to shore
> At full moon.

Some of these lesser similes however, though having only one tenor, have more than one analogue, causing the reader to make up tenors which may not be necessary or even relevant. Rustum is wounded and Ruksh his horse screams:

> ... most like the roar
> Of some pain'd desert-lion, who all day
> Hath trail'd the hunter's javelin in his side
> And comes at night to die upon the sand.
>   (503-506)

Here we can say that the simile doubles itself: Ruksh symbolises Rustum's agony, and both are like a wounded lion (Rustum by Sohrab's sword, Ruksh by sympathy) – but the problem is that neither die. There are too many analogues for the one tenor, and we have to assume Arnold is more concerned with Homeric ecphrasis than strict analogy.

Such lesser similes are signalled by 'as' or more usually 'like.' The extended similes however are perfectly enclosed ("as ... so" or "like ... so"), as if to remind the reader that the simile is finished; the lesser similes are not enclosed, on the presumption that the reader can hold the relationship of analogue to tenor without strain.

Are these extended similes effective? Here Rustum watches the advancing Sohrab:

> As some rich woman, on a winter's morn,
> Eyes through her silken curtains the poor drudge
> Who with numb blacken'd fingers makes her fire –
> At cock-crow on a starlit winter's morn,
> When the frost flowers the whiten'd window-panes –
> And wonders how she lives, and what the thoughts
> Of that poor drudge may be; so Rustum eyed
> ... and wonder'd who he was.
>   (302-308)

There are only two direct similarities here, morning and wonderment; the discrepancies are serious:

- rich lady and poor drudge imply a mistress/servant relationship, at odds with the heroic equality of Rustum and Sohrab;

- what are the tenors for silken curtains and whiten'd window-panes?
- eyelashes and glazed eyes do not befit a hero, and in any case nothing obstructs Rustum's view of Sohrab, who surely can hardly be likened to a poor drudge. Many of the long similes show like discrepancies. But having said that, many similes are strictly analogous, such as the beautiful one at lines 672-677:

TENOR		ANALOGUE
Sohrab's mother in Aderbaijan	=	*Cunning workman, in Pekin*
Pricks the griffin sign	=	*Pricks with vermilion*
Sohrab's white skin	=	*clear porcelain vase*
Rustum's son	=	*emperor's gift*
Love and toil of mother	=	*studious forehead and thin hands*

On the whole, however, we must say that the similes are more Homeric than Miltonic: they are marvellously relevant to the time and place of the action; they act as decorative digressions; they sum up the underpinning idea of the tenor; they are not, though, proleptic nor strictly analogous. They are descriptive ecphrases and fulfil his critical standards of what he felt the qualities of epic to be.

The epic features that Arnold uses in 'Sohrab and Rustum' are listed with their line numbers as follows:

- Hero's Food (196-199)
- The Catalogue of Towns and Heroes (110-135, of which lines 110-116 comprise a simile; 136-140; 747-766)
- The Heroic Wish (49-54; 236-241)
- The Heroic Funeral (783-805)
- Armour Description (265-269; 408-416)
- The Heroic Boast (325-329; 369-372; 433-435; 459-468; 528-539; 542-547)
- The Giving of Gifts (353-361)
- Magic or the Supernatural (481-490; lines 499-507 mirror the *Iliad*'s reference to Achilles' speaking horse; lines 658-691, Sohrab's proof of birth, allude to Odysseus' describing the marriage-bed to Penelope).

The main extended similes are to be found in lines 110-16; 160-9; 284-90; 302-8; 314-18; 390-97; 410-15; 472-8; 556-74; 634-8; 672-7; and 860-4. It is this lack of control over his similes and the sheer amount of them that ultimately disappoints, but there is no denying that many are truly satisfying as objects of beauty in themselves.

The Arnoldian simile works if we say that it takes a different direction to both the Homeric and Miltonic simile, but fails when we cannot relate it to one or the other. Arnold's failure was that he switched between all three where the general reader is literate only in one type (the Miltonic). He should not only have developed his own version but used only it.

What is this Arnoldian simile? Odysseus strings a rope across his courtyard from which to hang his traitorous handmaidens:

> ... then, like doves caught in a thicket where they come to roost and meeting death where they had only looked for sleep, the women held their heads out in a row and a noose was cast round each one's neck to despatch them.
>
> (Bk XXII, 467 on)

Of course, birds do not offer themselves for death, the hand-maidens do. The problem (to us, not the ancients) with the analogy here is one of action – to Homer the strung rope suggests a bird-net, and he proceeds to give the bird-net a life of its own, unrelated to the tenor of the passage. The Homeric simile takes us out of the event. The Arnoldian simile, however, brings us into the event by concentrating on the single object as opposed to Homerically expanding from it. Rustum siezes his club:

> ... like those which men in treeless plains
> To build them boats fish from the flooded rivers
> Hyphasis or Hydraspes, when, high up
> By their dark springs, the wind in winter-time
> Hath made in Himalayan forests wrack,
> And strewn the channels with torn boughs – so huge
> The club which Rustum lifted now.
>
> (410-416)

There is no action here, the tenor of the huge club returns to itself. In between, however, we have the description – a possible history – of the club. The simile is of an object, and the analogue is then continued in additions that refer to the analogue, not the tenor. This contrasts with Miltonic usage, where simile customarily consists of action, each succeeding analogue being required to refer to the tenor.

Another aspect of the Arnoldian simile is that it also supplies integral features of the epic structure: the simile of the two eagles in line 472 not only describes the heroic fight but moves into a second simile that is resonant of Homeric homeliness (woodcutters in the forest); this second simile also serves to describe the hero's armour.

By contrast, Tennyson's epyllion the 'Morte D'Arthur' contains only two similes, the longest right at the end in a prominent and evocative position, a total of just five lines out of less than 250.

Whether we consider Arnold's use of the simile to work or not we cannot ignore 'Sohrab and Rustum's superb ending (lines 875-892). As in 'The Scholar-Gypsy' the poem's ending sums up the theme and lifts the poem into an allusive world, but unlike 'The Scholar-Gypsy' this ending (or coda, defined as an addition to a basic structure) is much more tightly controlled; and not being introduced as a simile relieves it of any analogous constriction. For it could easily be prefaced by "But his soul, like the majestic river, floated on", thus making it an extended simile. It is this last point – that it is not a simile – that gives the coda such fine magicality and strength. Its symbolic power is such that we cannot read this section without moving beyond its immediately obvious allegory (the passing of Sohrab's soul, or the life of man in general, with its thematic similarity to his 1852 poem 'The Future' which is concerned with the river of time, the murmurs and scents of the infinite sea) into a universe of meaningful possibilities.

Whereas we could say that simile comprises tenor and analogue in dependent story lines, the last section of 'Sohrab and Rustum' takes on an independent life of its own, beyond its overt descriptiveness. The section moves in parallel to the preceding story-line and is linked to it by a bridging paragraph, but it exists as if in another dimension – it is both an outgrowth of the poem and of its own generation, and these give it its outstanding poetic effect.

How is this power achieved? Put simply, the poem's plot suggests the theme of its coda, and the bridge (the intervening paragraph) between plot and coda not only concentrates the plot but launches the coda into that nebulous world of possibilities between simile and allegory. This process can be broken down as follows:

The plot of lines 1-864 tells the basic story of Sohrab's fight with and killing by Rustum, his unwitting father. Noticeably, words that have an innate symbolic value independent of any context – fog, water, sands, night – provide a natural background to the plot.

The bridging section of lines 865-874 repeats the backgound of sands, river, night and fog, but because of their independent symbolism these references now dissolve the physical background into a mental backdrop.

The coda of lines 875-892 takes us finally from the physical background, "Out of the mist ... Into the frosty starlight" which now dots our mental backdrop. As if undergoing an out-of-body experience, we are both above and yet part of the mighty river that after many wanderings floats us through that backdrop into "a luminous home ... bright/ And tranquil."

The ending takes on a life of its own, as if the poem has given birth to another self, and lifts the action into the world of the mythopoeic, an effect of the imagination the simile could not achieve. This lifting of the poem is comparable to the attempt at the end of 'The Scholar-Gypsy' to raise the poem to another dimension, but there the simile construction leaves us floating, still attached to its main-frame; in 'Sohrab and Rustum' we are launched like Sohrab's soul into another world.

'Balder Dead' (1855)

The poem comprises three parts, telegraphically entitled: *I. Sending, II. Journey to the Dead, III. Funeral*, of 342, 310 and 565 lines respectively, over 300 longer than 'Sohrab and Rustum'.

The title is influenced by Milton's syntactical quirk in creating the title "Paradise Lost": not just the Latinate noun-adjective construction fit for an epic modelled on classical lines, but also as a linguistic shorthand to express more than one idea – an unfindable paradise that is also a paradise that human sin has forfeited. Balder has not only died – he has been made dead by treachery and evil, and it is this morally doomed otherworld, this Balder dead, that suffuses the whole poem.

Milton was fond of linguistic short cuts, especially syntactic and etymological, using words in both their original and current sense to show how far Satan had fallen from the original Prince of Light and mankind from paradise (in Bk I, line 146, Satan falls "with hideous ruine and combustion down", where "ruine" has not only the Carolian – and modern – sense of toppled or shattered, but also the original Latin sense of falling).

In his critiques Arnold does not mention Milton's linguistic style (though in 'Thyrsis' the reference to "silly sheep" may show its influence), but he was certainly aware of Milton's use of the verse paragraph (a sentence strung out for the length of a paragraph): "so chary of a sentence is he, so resolute not to let it escape him till he has crowded into it all he can" (*On Translating Homer*). The influence of the Miltonic verse paragraph is slight, the most obvious example being *II* 47-69 where Arnold compresses the completion of a series of related actions into a stand-alone paragraph. Although not strung out over a single sentence, the Miltonic effect is achieved through Arnold's use of the paratactic with its exponential increase of the number of ands – "till he has crowded into it all he can".

Arnold is more indebted in his use of Miltonic structure and style. We see it structurally in the use of exposition. As in both *Paradise Lost* and *Paradise Regained* this is at once immediate and proleptic (the past and future implicit or explicit in the present). Within the first eight lines of 'Balder Dead', a minor Miltonic verse-paragraph, the past cause is explained, the present action defined and the future doom implicit in the reference to Lok. The future becomes explicit 20 lines later (*I* 28-33), where Odin's speech is both expositional and proleptic, looking forward to Balder's vision of the twilight of the gods in *III* 487-498 and its aftermath of hope in the closing lines of the poem (*III* 510-42, the second Asgard). Noticeably Arnold is careful not to make it a prophecy of the Christian heaven. The alternative version of divine history is given by Hela, Queen of Hell in *II* 206-224 – the past defeat of Fenris and his children, their present pain, their future hope of victory. As in Satan's rousing speech in Book II of *Paradise Lost* it is a dramatic counterbalance to the accepted view of what should be.

Milton's latinate style is much in evidence in Arnold's use of the adjective-noun construction in oral-formulaic phrases. Examples are: "his horse Sleipner" (*I* 47), "the boar Serimner" (*I* 67, III 210), "the bridge Bifrost" (*I* 141, III 216), "the ash Igdrasil" (*II* 33, *III* 217), "the hall Gladheim" (*II* 36), and of course 'Balder Dead'. A similar Miltonicism that ultimately derives from Homer is place-naming, some of which in their repetition also serve as oral-formulas: "Fensaler stands, the house" (*I* 84) and "his mother's house,/ Fensaler" (*I* 197-8); "his own house,/ Breidablik" (*I* 207-8, and *III* 449); "Bifrost, where is Heimdall's watch" (*I* 141 and *II* 22); "the hill of Lidskialf" (*I* 253), "the wood/ Of Jarnvid"(*III* 329-30) and so on.

Milton's use of syntactic displacement to wind a long sentence back to its centre, especially with regard to appositional phrases – a stylistic quirk that can trace its roots back to *Beowulf* – is much less in evidence. The only example I can find is: "As wholly to be pitied, quite forlorn" (*III* 458), where the phrase refers back to "me" (Balder) two lines before. However, Miltonic and Marlovian lines are echoed throughout, and the reader will find them readily apparent if not occasionally ironic.

Clough described the poem as written "in the neo-Homeric manner" by which, presumably, he meant according to "the grand style" of Homer as perceived by Arnold. Besides plainness and elevated subject-matter Homer's influence is seen in Arnold's use of the oral formula. This repetitive rhythmic phrase is firstly a basic character description for the audience to remember who's who (or what's what) in a multititude of characters, and secondly a rhythmic foot or longer with which the poet can mechanically complete a line – an economic shortcut to composition whilst reciting. The same oral formula may be shared by many poets across many poems; in such cases it functioned as a ritualistic affirmation of communal identity. In *The Epic of Gilgamesh*, oral formula serves more as an action-retake, this repetition acting like a sling to suddenly throw the epic movement forward at moments of tension. On a lower level it is a mnemonic device to remind a Sumerian audience in their cups of what they have just missed.

I have already mentioned some types of oral formula such as "Sleipner, Odin's horse" (*I* 138, *I* 169, *II* 115 and *II* 147), but the

Homeric oral formula as character description is used sparingly if obviously: "Balder, so loved a God" (*I* 22 and *I* 26), Hoder as "the blind Hoder" (*I* 72 and *I* 131) or "a child of bale" (*I* 95 and *I* 112). Such scarcity does not allow them the cumulative effect of the most powerful of those in Homer which, by the end, have gathered up so many related connotations that they can almost stand alone from their original referent and become emblems of the epic theme. In all senses, everything at the close of *The Odyssey* – the shipwrecks, bloodletting, halls of feasting, drownings, isles, magic and murder – is wine-dark as the sea that embraced their every action.

The use of oral formula was superseded by literature i.e. by what was written down as a memory bypass, though literate poets like Vergil and the early medieval poets continued to use it as epic signature (or epic pretense). The formulaic description was possibly an attempt to come closer to the essence of what we are, the unique summation of what each artifact object and form in the world represents. The implication is that the formula encapsulates a universal truth. This association with the Platonic ideal may explain the volume of the formulaic and iconographic in medieval poetry and renaissance art, when Plato was much admired, Botticelli's *The Three Graces* or *The Birth of Venus* being obvious types. Just as the iconography of these paintings looks to the Platonic ideal so too does Milton's use of language in *Paradise Lost* – a searching for the semantic core behind each word, from their modern debasement to their original meaning. Such visual formulae as Botticelli's have extended their range. In films for example a still image of Parliament is a shortcut to saying "this is Britain", and is not to be taken as a live image or even relevant to the storyline it introduces or London as the place of action. In such stereotyped scene-pointers the characters are absent to reinforce the generalised message. Where the specific such as an individual is placed in the context of the iconographic formula we presume a truth from its proxy, a trick with which Arnold experiments in 'Balder Dead' and perfects in 'Thyrsis'. So the image of Kate Adie in front of a tank tells us "oh God, another civil war somewhere" – an economy of costs is achieved by not showing the moving stream of action before the narrator's eyes, because what supposedly is happening offscreen she verbalises in front of its signifier, the tank. In such cases history becomes the imaginative masquerading as the factual it pretends to illustrate.

We find this in 'Balder Dead' in Arnold's use of simile, where the tenor (the action referred to) is not just represented by but integrated into its analogue (object of likeness). This goes beyond the BBC's substitution of imagination for reality, by merging the two into an otherness of aesthetic reality.

Arnold's use of the simile in 'Balder Dead' both differs from, and extends, his use of it in 'Sohrab and Rustum'. The similes are much fewer – only 11 – and much more dispersed than in 'Sohrab and Rustum'. They amount to 83 lines (or 88 if we include the five short similes such as "like eddying leaves" (*I* 177) or "like a young child" (*I* 291)) out of a total of 1217 lines, or 1 in 14, almost half the ratio of the earlier epyllion. Perhaps Arnold was hoping to achieve a greater impact by their rarer use; more likely he had become sensitive to criticism of his over-use of them in 'Sohrab and Rustum'. But, importantly, his experimentation with the simile continues. Of the 11, two – *II* 91-99 and *III* 8-19 – collapse under their ineptness, and two are excellent – *III* 357-68 with its melancholic metaphor of the thwarted homecoming and *III* 306-317, where the tenor/analogue relationship is exactly balanced yet displays increasing signs of integration. There are two other similes in the poem where this integration of analogue to tenor is even more obvious, further reinforced by their shortness, to such an extent that similitude and sameness become almost indistinguishable. This is an important divergence in the literary use of the simile and I shall look at these three in detail.

The first concern's Hermod's return from hell:

> And as a traveller in the early dawn
> To the steep edge of some great valley comes,
> Through which a river flows, and sees, beneath,
> Clouds of white rolling vapours fill the vale,
> But o'er them, on the farther slope, descries
> Vineyards, and crofts, and pastures, bright with sun –
> So Hermod, o'er the fog between, saw Heaven.
>
> (*II* 295-301)

Across the abysmal snow-fog Hermod the traveller glimpses heaven; across the foggy valley the traveller glimpses the Arcadian hamlet. The analogue here is so exact as to be not a likeness of its tenor but the thing itself. The sunny crofts and vines defended by fog (an image of the otherworld in both Germanic and Celtic mythology) have moved effortlessly from the earthly pastoral to the eternity of heaven. Heaven and earth become integrated, the gods are both gods and men, and for a moment we glimpse with Hermod the future beyond Ragnarok – the fading of godhead and the ascent of man.

In the second simile Balder's funeral pyre is slowly dousing itself:

> And as, in a decaying winter fire,
> A charr'd log, falling, makes a shower of sparks –
> So with a shower of sparks the pile fell in,
> Reddening the sea around; and all was dark.
> (*III* 203-6)

The tenor of the funeral pyre is the same as its analogue of the winter fire of charred logs, for the one could just as easily be described in terms of the other, giving the impression that the death of Balder has become the death of its every earthly similitude – "and all was dark". This is not only proleptic of the coming twilight of the gods but consciously apt, for Balder was the god of light and the longer days of spring.

The last of these three similes (*III* 307-18) is not so immediate in its impact, taking seven lines for the analogue to appear as its own tenor. The analogue of winter thawing takes three lines to appear – "And as ... a dripping sound is heard" (*III* 307/310) – then expands into a description of the approach of spring amidst snows melted round patches of growing grass, ending with:

> So through the world was heard a dripping sound
> Of all things weeping to bring Balder back
> (*III* 317-18)

The weeping world (the tenor) is not only like melting winter, it becomes it in expectation of Balder's return, of the coming of spring. But this is deep proleptic irony, for the audience knows that all things did not weep to bring Balder back; they wept in pity for Balder who was doomed to endure in hell. He and we remain in winter, in coldness and eternal melting with no sign of the rebirth we yearn for. Nothing could be further from Homeric, ecphrasis or closer to the epic theme.

Arnold is thus experimenting again with the simile, but as opposed to his experiments in 'Sohrab and Rustum', where the simile brings us into an event by concentrating on a single object or merges it into a succeeding one, in 'Balder Dead' he merges tenor and analogue within a single simile so that the mythopoeic world becomes as one with reality (as with the wine-dark sea consuming the whole 'Odyssey'). And where better than in heaven, in Asgard, to experiment with this, revealing his master's influence in his attempt to further the proleptic qualities of the Miltonic simile.

I can't help but feel however that 'Balder Dead' remains an experiment, not carried through in every innovative case, not excisive of its failures (the anti-climax of Hoder's death, the repetitive journeys into hell), and unsure finally of its stylistic direction. But Arnold was to explore successfully the poem's analogous potential in 'Thyrsis', as we shall see, by means of extracting the symbolic core from the simile and allowing it to represent at once itself, its meaning and its context.

3

Arnold as Critic

"The Child is Father of the Man", wrote Wordsworth, one of Arnold's life-long mentors. And certainly in Arnold's case his character – the offspring of experience and belief – plays almost as important a part in the formulation of his critical theories as does pure study and intellectual pursuit.

Character and beliefs

The Cornish element in Arnold's blood (his mother was Mary Penrose, a Cornishwoman) has been seen by some as explaining Matthew's temperament of melancholy juxtaposed against a wilful jauntiness; more likely he regarded her Celticness as an ally in his struggle to overturn his father's influence purely because of its imagined non-Englishness. By extension whatever was culturally (but not politically) non-English also became an ally. Dr Thomas Arnold's personality was strong, prejudicial, emphatic, energetic, of a high moral rectitude, prone to wrath and even perhaps somewhat paranoiac. As Murray says, he "translated the most trivial events in everyday life … into adventures in righteousness." But he also had a happy domestic side to him and loved playing with his children. Paradoxically it may have been his father's Englishness, his rejection of the subjective and irrelevant, his stern idealism and unswerving, almost ruthless, drive towards that idealism, that helped formulate Arnold's two famous critical tenets – that the artist should concentrate on high seriousness and on what was eternal and profound in human experience. This paradox may also explain why Arnold turned in the late 1850s (ironically whilst Professor of Poetry at Oxford) from writing poetry to writing criticism – his romantic and therefore in his own mind, Celtic capriciousness could never harmonise with the classical and thus English seriousness of matter and style he demanded in others.

He produced his best work – the elegies and melancholic poems – when he refused to allow his critical ideals to interfere with his creative processes: as he wrote to Clough, "a slight gift of poetical expression which in a common person might have developed itself easily and naturally, is overlaid and crushed in a profound thinker." Pompous and true, but purposefully ironised in typical Arnoldian vein with the pretense of laconicism. According to Clough, Arnold was distrustful of strong-minded writers with a design upon the reader, preferring Keats' negative capability, "a general torpor, with here or there a laughing or crying philosopher." In December 1847 he had savaged some of Clough's poems, comparing him to his bugbear Tennyson: "to solve the universe as you try to do is as irritating as Tennyson's dawdling with its painted shell."

His correspondence with Clough at this time hints at his growing belief that the response to the world by modern poets was bound to be different to that of past poets – the modern age, being more complex with more awareness of pressures, was a greater challenge to the poet. By 1869 Arnold could write to his mother that "my poems represent, on the whole, the main movement of mind of the last quarter of a century … I have less poetical sentiment than Tennyson, and less intellectual vigour and abundance than Browning … I have perhaps more of a fusion of the two than either of them, and have more regularly applied that fusion to the main line of modern development." The "main movement of mind" is presumably the zeitgeist. In his letters to Clough, Arnold wrote that the austerity of his verse mirrored the time's "blankness and barrenness and unpoetryness;" "Congestion of the brain is what we suffer from," "Arid – that is what the times are."

The Doctor died on 12th June 1842, aged 46, of angina whilst his son was studying at Balliol. Matthew was warned that the action of his own heart was not regular and that he might die early of a similar cause. This possibility was to haunt him for the rest of his life. Released from his father's powerful personality he may have been (as described in 'Rugby Chapel'), but its influence long remained. Arnold became more bantering in his attitudes, with an "exuberant versatile nature", as his brother Tom described him, and dressed fashionably. Goethe now displaced Byron as his poetic mentor. Though he was meant to be studying Divinity, Latin, Greek, Logic, Morals and Mathematics, his attendance was desultory and "not sufficiently attentive to the rules of the College." He felt no desire to partake in the Tractarian debates convulsing the Anglican Church, not even for the intellectual satisfaction.

Besides indolence, a problem for Arnold was his dry sense of humour, deadpan, laconic at the wrong times; it was misunderstood by his friends and he often declined to be taken seriously when it was most expected of him. He was becoming a dilettante, dressy, fond of the hunt, and his studies suffered. This idleness, reinforced by a belief that his own inventiveness and talent were all that were needed to gain him a 1st class degree, resulted in Balliol's awarding him a 2nd in November 1844. He became a temporary master at Rugby, being frequently late for chapel and playing a great deal of billiards and whist. His notebooks show his interest in philosophy (Plato, Kant, Mill, Berkeley, St Augustine, Descartes) possibly to bolster his growing agnosticism.

Unsure of his Christianity, and having no philosophy save that of an ambiguous trust in an ideal culture, he could not sing his beliefs, only his despair. Nor could he be detached enough – or feel himself able to be detached – from his uneasiness with modern life to write objectively about ideas or emotions, as he considered Milton (another alienated poet) able to do.

His intellectual idleness may be to blame; he had to force himself – and Clough had to force him – to both study and write. Charlotte Brontë considered (she met him on the 21st December 1850 at Fox Howe) that "a real modesty appeared under his assumed conceit, and some genuine intellectual aspirations ... displaced superficial affectations." Of her he said "past thirty and plain, with expressive gray eyes though." Anti-sexists will be pleased to note that whereas Brontë's description is cerebral, that of Arnold is merely physical. But whose is the more immediate? And don't the gray eyes tell us Arnold saw something of Marguerite in Charlotte? Certainly he could be a fop and somewhat pretentious – and certainly he played upon this for his own delight. The rakish life appealed to him: whilst on holiday in Brighton in 1854 he played cards and drank champagne till cockcrow with officers of the 17th Lancers, their depot being commanded by Flu's brother-in-law. The appeal of such dissoluteness excused by duty may have urged him to join the Queen's Westminster Rifle Volunteers – the Pimlico Rifles – as a volunteer in August 1859, but only for two or three nights a week.

After his visit to George Sand at Nohant in 1846 he became a Francophile, to Clough's disgust. "It is the Norman element in England which has kept her from getting stupid and humdrum." Such outrageous statements reflect more on his temperament than his intellect. His over-eager Francophilia (the nearest refuge of anti-English sensibilities, as every Scotsman with an *Ecosse* car-sticker knows) blinded him to the immense possibilities of the energy and power that were permeating every aspect of British life, spiritual as well as economic. An energy which had both repelled and attracted Blake, "colossal and unparallelled" as Engels described it. "To France I have always felt myself powerfully drawn. People in England often accuse me of liking France and things French far too well," he admits in *Discourses in America*. This Francophilia narrowed him into a European world opposed to the mondial outlook of his own country. In many ways Europe had become politically outdated, even sidelined, spending itself in barren intellectualism and the erection of cultural ideals that had little to do with the economic reality of the global village Britain was forcing onto the world.

Industrialisation

With the increasing advance of science and industry and the vast plains of bricks and smoking chimneys that spread over Britain after 1760 the world must indeed have seemed spiritually dead. The rape of nature, land clearances, forced emigration (whether to the colonies or the great cities), the death of local customs and even of whole villages, was finally crowned in 1859 with the triumph of evolution and the death of God. And the touchstone of this new civilisation was Manchester.

Between 1770 and 1831 Manchester, 'symbol of a new age' as Asa Briggs describes it in *Victorian Cities*, increased its population six times, "the din of its machinery being the music of economic progress." In the filth of materialism and agony of spiritual suffering both Blake's *Jerusalem* and Dickens' *Hard Times* took their inspiration from industrialisation, attracted to its repulsiveness and repulsed by its inexorability. Others were quite open in their admiration for the new age: Manchester was described by *Chambers' Edinburgh Journal* in 1858 as "the very symbol of civilisation;" "The age of ruins is past ... have you seen Manchester?" is asked in Disraeli's *Coningsby* of 1844; to Carlyle, Cottonopolis was "as wonderful ... as unimaginable, as the oldest Salem or prophetic city." The 'Manchester School', a term coined by Gladstone in 1846, dominated world economic thinking, expressing itself through *The Manchester Times*, the announcer to the old world of what this new world was and thought. Mrs Gaskell's *Mary Barton*, 1848, is sub-titled *A Tale of Manchester Life*. Manchester, ironically, became a symbol of urban as opposed to pastoral romance, still hinted at today in TV's *Coronation Street*. Engels romanticised it even further – his shocking descriptions of its filth, smoke and slum-dwellers hid an admiration for its sheer energy and promise: he urged Marx to visit the city and the result was *The Communist Manifesto* of 1848 and later *Das Kapital* (1867), an injection of Manchester economic practice into the aging but still emotional politics of the French Revolution. Here was the furnace wherein the urban proletariat would be forged into the harbingers of the Golden City.

With the death of God came the end of Christian history; the new era was felt to be heralded by Manchester and its offspring, but the problem was one of defining it. The fact of God was to be replaced by the theory of economic progress whereby man would evolve into a superior being whose perfection would be expressed by Utopia, the end of history. Notice that like the basis of other new sciences and arts of the time, evolutionary theory was seen as the answer to every doubt and the starting point of each new hypothesis. Man was not special to creation and no longer had a goal or even meaning to his life, save the nebulous one of progress that replaced the Christian march to heaven, at the whim of the material prosperity that Manchester represented and which further increased his dependency and degradation. Marx coined the term 'capitalism' for this cycle of economic dependency, where investors were supposedly immune because of the return on their capital but the real producers of the goods – the working class – were those who suffered the most.

But his theory was contested by Christian revivalists, 'fellow travellers', social anthropologists and economic theorists. Each succeeding generation found itself at the mercy of any fashionable social theory that dragged the idea of progress into a new direction. "Wandering between two worlds, one dead/The other powerless to be born" ('Stanzas from the Grande Chartreuse'). To thinkers like Arnold man had become perverted from a being a natural symbol of God to a uniform symbol of the dominant ideology, whose sole function was to play out the stereotype of class or economy or race, further depriving him of any individuality, or worse, of any other meaning in life. Maybe this pessimistic view of 'progress' was justified – mankind's only spiritual relief in the 20th century has been to find its individual worth by partaking in the mass despair of Auschwitz, the Gulag and the Somme: "And the individual withers and the world is more and more" ('Locksley Hall'), wrote Tennyson prophetically.

In 1841 Arnold went up to Balliol College; in 1851 he became an Inspector of Schools. In between were the 'hungry forties', a decade of economic and political turmoil. Hearts hardened by Malthusianism became inured to the horrors of the Irish famine and the iniquity of the corn laws. Chartism was rife in the great cities. It was therefore no accident that it was also a decade of great socio-economic commentary: in 1844 Engels published *The Condition of the Working Class in England* (English edition 1892) and 1848 was a watershed in such publishing – *The Communist Manifesto* by Marx and Engels, Mrs Gaskell's *Mary Barton* with its furious attack on the Manchester mill-owners of the time (Arnold admired her work and sent her copies of his poems), and of course *The Principles of Political Economy* by John Stuart Mill. Abroad, Europe witnessed tremendous upheavals in the crushing of revolution in Prussia, and the overthrow of Metternich in Austria and the monarchy in France. But in 1851, along with Arnold's inspectorship, came the Great Exhibition of Britain's wealth, power and industry and its ushering in of 30 years of immense prosperity.

During this time Arnold described himself as a Liberal. In 'To A Republican Friend, 1848', the friend is Clough, and the poem claims to support his republican views – "God knows it, I am with you", though this opening statement makes us ask why Arnold is having to justify himself. 'Continued' (1849) carries straight on from the previous sonnet, but starts to back-peddle from its "what you feel, I share" to its "Yet, when I muse … I seem … to patience prompted." Practicality overcomes enthusiasm and Utopia is not round the corner ("nor will that day dawn at human nod"). Arnold is more concerned with showing the reality of mankind than in enforcing Chartist revolution. "I should be sorry to live under their government," he told his mother, "nor do I intend to."

It was the principles of economics and their effects on every aspect of life that Arnold refused to come to terms with. He turned to a Europe that might yet be saved from the British revolution. Unable to become the new Goethe putting his finger on Europe's ills, he retreated into an intellectualism that could only watch society's upheavals and dynamism without becoming part of it save by a criticism consisting of sensibility without heroic action. Some of his social observations were acute: in a letter to Clough he said "the world tends to become more comfortable for the mass, and more uncomfortable for those of any natural gift or distinction." A note of self-pity here there may be, but also an honest awareness of the levelling and materially beneficial aspects of the Industrial Revolution. And of its spiritlessness and dumbing down, too.

This then was the dilemma that faced every writer – indeed every educated person – of the mid-Victorian age, and resulted from the dichotomy of the industrial city. "The great town's harsh, heart-wearying roar" ('Thyrsis', 234) was a symbol both of prosperity and despair – should we force ourselves to see a golden dawn behind the smoke and the stench, or reclaim before it was too late a less sensitive, but nobler, world of the past?

Parnassus & Parnassians

From industrialisation's present reality Arnold escaped to the haven of aestheticism, whence he felt secure enough to make such evaluations as that of Tennyson's 'Maud' (published in 1855): "intensely provincial, not European." So what was this European cultural ideal he was increasingly being drawn towards?

Keats had proposed that there is an aesthetic sense by which we appreciate the beautiful, a sense independent of morality and intellect. If so, the artist works through this special sense, and the German philosopher Kant put forward an aesthetic theory whereby moral and intellectual standards have no place in the appreciation of art. A work of art had therefore purposefulness but no purpose, like the lilies of the field, and could only be judged by its own implicit rules. Just as art had been perceived as freeing itself in classical times from religion, so it was now perceived with the advent of Darwinism as having freed itself from morality. This mix produced in England the idea of 'Art for art's sake' and was enthusiastically adopted by Swinburne and Pater, whose *Studies in the History of the Renaissance* became the Parnassians' rule-book.

Parnassian was a term coined in 1866 (the year of writing 'Thyrsis') by a group of French poets for the periodical in which they published their work, *Le Parnasse Contemporain*. Parnassus, the abode of Apollo and the Muses, represented artistic constraint and was opposed to 19th century materialism and Romantic frenzy; extreme Parnassians went further and attacked Christianity and the notion of literature as edification. In particular they stood for:

- Poetic emotional control
- Severity of form (objectivity, restraint, strict adherence to form)
- Beauty as an independent value (art for art's sake)

But this attempt to introduce art for art's sake under a classical guise wilfully ignored the moral intent of classical art. Current ethical standards could thus be rejected – both Swinburne and Wilde upheld the Parnassian doctrine that art has nothing to do with sexual morality and used art to advance a new sexual morality whilst ostensibly appealing to the supposed ideals of classical art.

Parnassian writers were deeply read in the classics. But they did not limit their imaginations to the classical past, nor deny the middle ages or the present – they were eclectic, "part of a new sense of history" as Highet says, begun by Gibbon and Niebuhr, and diffused into the public consciousness. Scientific intrusion into the field of the arts led to a more sceptical but more accurate reconstruction of history. But the myth of classical civilisation was too strong to be discarded – it was deeply felt to be a nobler world than that created by the Industrial Revolution. So if the classical world was nobler, then its myths and heroes were held to be the more suitable role models for the expression of universal passions. As such, sexual themes could be openly expressed by isolating them in an imaginary classical world as in Browning's 'Fifine at the Fair', or Swinburne's 'Atalanta in Calydon'. Classical figures could also be used as personifications of the poet's internal conflicts as in Arnold's 'Empedocles on Etna' (1852). But Hellenism is not a normal part of everyday culture – the reference to Daphnis and Lityerses in 'Thyrsis' has to be explained in a note, and 'Merope' has to be prefaced with an explanation of the plot and its meaning.

In 'Empedocles on Etna' the eponymous hero, a poet and philosopher, has given up music and lives gloomily where "troubles confound the wit [that mankind] has." Callicles, a young poet, follows him at a distance up Etna. Where Empedocles is sceptical of an afterlife Callicles sings of the pleasures of experiencing nature. Empedocles recognises this difference and in despair throws himself into the volcano. There is no conflict between Empedocles and Callicles, and as a dramatic messenger Pausanias fails. There is little action, and Empedocles appears to have decided on his course of action before the poem begins. Although described as a dramatic poem, there is a great deal of soul-searching and moral commentary that smothers the action. There is some shrewd commentary on the world, but too much and too diffuse for what little action there is, too little tailored and edited for the theme. Empedocles and Callicles seem to represent Arnold's two selves, the thinker and the singer. Arnold saw Empedocles as a realist and agnostic, alienated by his beliefs from his fellow men, and thus a poet Arnold could empathise with; Callicles is a singer of nature and an optimist, an envied finder of meaning where Arnold was still searching. Empedocles accuses himself of being no slave to sense but slave to thought, a thought Arnold believed that crushes the bliss to be alive: he wrote to Clough that "I shall never have heat and radiance enough to pierce the clouds that are massed round me."

Anti-Christian attitudes had been apparent in Blake's extolling of pure energy as a goodness beyond principle, in Wordsworth's poetry of nature-worship, in Shelley's atheism and Byron's wilful rejection of religious morality. Attitudes hardened when extreme Parnassians accused Christianity of repression and impotence. What was felt to be tyranny and puritanism on the church's part had its compliment in what was assumed to be the freedom of paganism. For example, the Italian poet Carducci depicted Satan as the patron of human individuality oppressed by Catholicism. We have here an echo of Blake's comment that in *Paradise Lost* Milton was of the devil's party without knowing it. And repression included sexual repression – virginity and fasting – whereas classicism supposedly tolerated free love.

This repressiveness was assumed to be the result of an innate weakness in Christianity, a diffuse spirituality without a hard core to it. Paganism therefore was strong. Nietzsche, in his *Beyond Good and Evil*, believed that Greek art grew out of the tension between the barbaric forces of the frenzied Dionysus and his dithyrambic dances, and the calm beauty and reason of Apollo. The implication of this, he argued, was that Greek art is not cold, formal and structured but the product of violent conflict. Thus a dialectic of aestheticism was born from Darwinist evolutionary theory.

He also claimed that Christianity was an anti-Roman plot, dreamt up by the Jews as their revenge on the free pagan West, and then taken up by the early Church. The Jews were now portrayed as anti-Hellenistic barbarians belonging to a despotic orientalism not part of the European tradition. In Wilde's *Salome* for instance the Jews are portrayed as caricatures, further stereotyped by Strauss when he composed music for the play.

Was this defeatism, then, an escape from the horrors of the time? Most great writers have escaped – or at least appealed – to an imagined golden age, from the 'Gilgamesh' poet, through Hesiod and Malory to Dylan Thomas, even if only to end up in *The Waste Land*. To the Victorians the Classical world was seen as bright, warm, young, bursting with fecundity, full of imagination yet controlled by unchanging rituals and a sense of what was naturally proper (decorum). Pan's untutored music and Dionysus' drunken ecstatic poetry might terrify and make us marvel but still the god of harmony, Apollo, prevailed in the art-forms. Perhaps Arnold felt that artistically he was living in an age that could not better the 'classic' writers such as Shakespeare and Milton (much as Theocritus felt about his own times), and over time this made him turn more and more towards criticism.

The Inspector of Schools

"I should greatly have preferred to go to the colonies ... as colonial secretary or some such thing" he wrote to his brother Tom, who had worked in the Colonial Office before emigrating to New Zealand in 1847. His future father-in-law, Judge Wightman, was against it though, and the unenthusiastic Matthew became a schools inspector in 1851, marrying Fanny Wightman the following year.

Elementary schools only started to receive money after 1833, bringing education out of the fold of the Church and into that of government. Arnold was involved with this side of education – the universal compulsory state education whose effects, Arnold wrote prophetically to his sister Fan, would be seen in "civilising the next generation of the lower classes, who, as things are going, will have most of the political power of the country in their hands." Early in his career he had inspected schools in the Manchester area and admired the commitment of the great cotton manufacturers to an egalitarian approach to education, Manchester epitomising "a system of society constructed according to entirely new principles," as Murray says. His principal task was to inspect elementary schools which since 1839 had required inspection if they wished to maintain their state grants. Arnold would test, by written and *viva voce* examinations, pupils and pupil-teachers (older pupils who taught younger ones) at training colleges. In 1861 the Privy Council Committee on Education tried to introduce a new system for grant-aid schools – spending would be reduced by relating grants to the results of testing each pupil in reading, writing and arithmetic. Arnold opposed it; in his view the state should have "an interest in the primary school as a civilising agent, even prior to its interest in it as an instructing agent." In this he followed his father's precepts concerning public school education – moral integrity, Christian gentlemanliness, and intellectual ability. Such arguments about the philosophy of education still continue.

The Preface to the 1853 volume of poetry

The Preface is both a summation of previous critical remarks of Arnold, whether spoken or written, and a forerunner of his later theories on what poetry should be. It reveals his father's influence, not in its stern moral but in its stern aesthetic rectitude.

By the real Empedocles' time sophistry, the triumph of style over matter and morality, was dominant: "the calm, the cheerfulness, the disinterested objectivity have disappeared; the dialogue of the mind with itself has commenced... we hear already the doubts ... of Hamlet and of Faust." In such situations "no poetical enjoyment can be derived," for art should not only accurately represent but interest and "infuse joy". On this basis he disapproves of poetry where suffering finds no vent in action ... in which there is everything to be endured, nothing to be done," and thus 'Empedocles on Etna' was omitted from the volume because the hero's despair, Arnold now feels, was not a fit poetical theme.

Art, he wrote, should not necessarily concern itself with modern subjects, as some critics demanded. Arnold asks what are "the eternal objects of poetry ... ? They are actions; human actions; possessing an inherent interest in themselves ..." The representation of an inferior action is not ennobled by the poet's treatment of it, no matter how artistic. The greatest poetry belongs "to the domain of our permanent passions", for the most excellent action concerns "those elementary feelings ... which are independent of time." Past or present action, it makes no difference: Oedipus or Macbeth, the poet's "business is with their inward man." To the Greeks the "date of an action ... signifies nothing: the action itself, its selection and construction, this is what is all-important." But modern poets concern themselves with the action's "separate thoughts and images". The Greeks were masters of the grand style, regarding the whole and not the parts. Form and content were balanced in the careful construction of a poem, but to Arnold the modern poets had neglected the overall design in favour of "bursts of fine writing," and capriciousness.

This capriciousness was due to the "confusion of the present times," with its bewildering "multitude of voices counselling different things." The modern poet needs "a voice to prescribe to him the aim which he should keep in view," thus the appeal to Arnold of the formal restraint and objectivity of the classical poets.

Foremost among these voices is Shakespeare, a fitting model because "he knew well what constituted a poetic action" and because of his gift of ingenious expression. But here is the problem; it is this wonderful gift of expression that has been exclusively imitated and thus for modern poets "the details alone are valuable, the composition worthless." Structural clarity, calm pathos and simplicity of style are therefore best learned from the ancients. The result will be a "a unity and profoundness of moral impression" that will delight and instruct what is "permanent in the human soul."

Unfortunately an age of false pretensions, wanting in "moral grandeur" and sunk in "spiritual discomfort," cannot supply this, and Arnold refers us to the comments of Goethe and Niebuhr as evidence. The "boundaries and wholesome regulative laws" of the Greeks should be our guidelines, not their eternal enemy, the "caprice" of the Romantics.

In his very much shorter "Preface to the Second Edition" of 1854 Arnold defends his position, urging us to cure "the great vice of our intellect ... incredible vagaries in literature, in art, in religion, in morals: namely that it is fantastic, and wants sanity. Sanity – that is the great virtue of the ancient literature ..." Caprice is again the enemy.

Thus Arnold sets forth his definition and promotion of the grand style in poetry. Of course the implication is that British art lacks the stern paternal law of a French Academy, even if it may not miss it, and this need was later to be discussed in *Culture and Anarchy*.

On the Modern Element in Literature

In May 1857 Arnold was voted Professor of Poetry at Oxford by members of the Convocation. His duties were three lectures a year, a Latin oration every other year, and judging undergraduate prize poems, for £130 a year. Murray notes that he was the first holder of the post since its inception in 1708 not to be a clergyman; and he delivered his lectures in English not Latin, thus widening the debate about the role and constitution of poetry. His first lecture on 14th November 1857 was *On the Modern Element in Literature* – an attempt to impose his artistic standards on the poetry of the day. Sophocles was set up as a model of poetic style because he followed "the rule of reason, not ... the impulse of prejudice or caprice." It was to such a standard of poetry that Arnold tried to aspire in 'Merope'.

'Merope', a poetic drama ten years in the making, was published in December 1857. But most critics have panned it as a lifeless imitation of Sophocles' *Electra*. Arnold thought it satisfied the demands of his times and his own critical standards in its formal objectivity. The poem has a preface dealing with the choice of classical subject matter and its form and content. But Arnold had little sense of the truly dramatic (as previous poems had shown) and even less of basic stagecraft. Max-Müller, the critic, said of it: "I would wish you some English clouds – ay some London smoke – on the blue sky of your classical soul."

Reports on continental education

From March to August 1859 Arnold was sent as Foreign Assistant Commissioner on behalf of the Education Committee to Belgium, France and Switzerland. "I cannot tell you," he wrote to his sister, "how much I like the errand." It gave him an opportunity to indulge his Francophilia. His official report on continental education was published in 1861, a separate edition being published by Longman's as *Popular Education in France*. It failed to cover its costs. It was to form the basis of *A French Eton or Middle-Class Education and the State* (1864) in which Arnold lists the three classes – aristocracy, middle class and "populace" – and their effect on culture. Culture he argues is limited to the aristocracy only, and should be disseminated throughout the whole population by an educational system that was "reasonably cheap and reasonably good". State intervention, he believes, would redeem the middle class from its cultural mediocrity. He foresees its destiny as the dominant class in Britain, and his aim is to replace its materialism with a searching intellectualism before it "can have the right or power to assert itself absolutely". The Eton of the title was Toulouse Lyceum.

After another educational visit abroad in 1865-6, during which he was proud to be called a *Français* by the Parisian savants for his knowledge of French literature, his report on *Schools and Universities of the Continent* appeared in 1868. With a typical Arnoldian exhortation he urges the government to use the example of the continent's educational system to correct the Englishman's "ignorance of the right of mind and reason to rule human affairs."

On Translating Homer

The 20th century used the Sutton Hoo ship-burials as evidence of an historical Beowulf, and A.B. Lord's exploration of oral epic in the Balkans is still used to vindicate Homer's – and the Beowulf poet's

– use of repetition and formulaic epithet. But this trend is nothing new. Throughout the 19th century new scientific methods of study began to affect the traditional view of antiquity: linguists, historians, geologists, mathematicians, archaeologists, all reinterpreted the classics; the Homeric epics for instance were analysed in terms of Schiemann's finds at Mycenae and Troy. Academics began to specialise instead of giving an overview. New theories of translation were now put into practice. It was argued that besides being an excellent linguist the translator must be a fluent writer in his own language, and above all he must be knowledgeable in the field he is discussing.

In *On Translating Homer* (1861-62, from a series of Oxford lectures and essays), Arnold outlined what he considered the "true principles on which a translation of Homer should be founded." Because classical studies were in decline he felt it imperative that Homer be translated with as full a flavour of the original as possible. He attacked Francis Newman's pedantic translation of the *Iliad*; he brought Chapman, Pope, Cowper and others into the argument (their translations reflected the spirit of their own times and their own individuality), and emphasised that it is poetry, not mere words and grammar, that is at the heart of translation. As such the translation, like the original, should be in an elevated poetic style. In Highet's judgement Arnold "raised Homeric criticism out of the mass of pedantry ... and tastelessness into which it had been sinking." He argued against the view that the Homeric epics were sources of pre-classical Greek grammar or mere stimuli to (or confirmations of) archaeological discovery. If Homer was plain and direct in language any translation should also be. In fact Homer uses words that were obscure even in classical times, as well as mingling dialects in his grammar and syntax, and these pose extra problems for translators.

In his first lecture Arnold sets forth what he considers the essentials of 'the grand style' as found in Homer: rapidity of plot; plainness of style; simplicity of ideas; and nobility in manner – qualities Newman's translation had come nowhere near to, with his ballad-like style and quaint language. The grand style to Arnold was noble and edifying, refining "the raw natural man" within all of us. However, we should question whether Homer is as stylistically consistent as Arnold avers, or to what extent he even possesses these qualities.

In his second lecture he castigated English literature of his own time as hardly a "living intellectual instrument" because literature in Britain was regarded as merely an object of interest, and he indulged his weakness for ranking by placing English literature after German and French. But we have to ask, is great literature an intellectual or aesthetic achievement? If aesthetic, it is art for art's sake and beyond Arnold's strictures; if intellectual, what price his earlier appeal to poetic sensibility? Arnold came down on the side of mental lucidity and this, he argues, is what is lacking in Homeric translations. It was about this time he made his famous remark that Tennyson was "deficient in intellectual power." In his turn, Tennyson said of dining with Arnold that he "didn't much like dining with Gods!"

In his third lecture Arnold stated that the hexameter was the best way of translating the rhythm of Homer into English; it had a "natural dignity" and a "loose grammatical style". But here Arnold stands accused by his own opinion, of analysing the past not in its own terms but in those of the current mind-set. In such an analysis, criticising English verse rhythms in terms of Greek poetics, his belief in literature as an "intellectual instrument" reveals itself not as objective criticism but as the natural prejudice of his age. He had experimented with translating Homer into English hexameters, but as he himself admitted, had failed. That should have told him pure entertainment can be art but pure art cannot be entertainment. Artistic theory is wedded to its object of study, and once divorced from it – as in art for art's sake – it is no longer criticism but merely another work of art.

On 30th November, two weeks after the death of Clough, he delivered his "last word" on Homer, regretting the strength of his attack on Newman and that there was no literary academy in Britain to deliver a "final judgement" on literary debates, to control "false tendencies" and "eccentric theories", and urging that the critic of poetry should have "the finest tact, the nicest moderation, the most free, flexible and elastic spirit imaginable." The lecture ended with a reference to Clough as one who never degraded himself, in the struggle for literary recognition, "in the saturnalia of ignoble passions." His life in this respect, he said, was one of "Homeric simplicity".

His demands of the literary critic are severe if not exorbitant, but at least Arnold tried to put his theories into practice in his two attempts at composing epic poetry (one should really call them epyllions), 'Sohrab and Rustum' and 'Balder Dead'.

On The Study of Celtic Literature

In 1852 Arnold was inspecting Welsh schools, noting that they taught Welsh. He agreed that Welsh should be encouraged for "philological or antiquarian interest", but that the state should force (by the lever of grant-aid) the use of English on them to eliminate social and linguistic divisions within the kingdom. In 1859, though he knew none of its languages, he started exploring Celtic literature: "We owed far more, spiritually and artistically, to the Celtic races than the somewhat coarse Germanic intelligence readily perceived," he wrote to his sister, with their Cornish mother (Mary Penrose) in mind. In August 1864 the family holidayed in north Wales: "the new race, language, and literature give it charm and novelty." "The poetry of the Celtic race ... quite overpowers me." He also liked the Celts' "melancholy and unprogressiveness". Arnold supported the right of the Irish to have a Catholic university, but in 1879 the government refused to endow one in Ireland for fear of upsetting the non-conformists.

Intellectually, Arnold may have despaired of his own nation, but politically he was fully in support of its internal and imperial policies. He felt that all the inhabitants of the British Isles should be "one homogeneous, English-speaking whole," and that separate provincial nationalities should be broken down: "the sooner the Welsh language disappears ... the better". Arnold saw the Philistines as the "guilty authors of Fenianism". He thus brings culture and politics into alliance, their single voice presumably to be expressed by a British literary academy whose function would be to provide a unifying ideology in both politics and the arts. In 1879 when the Zulu War was in progress, and a British army had been wiped out at Isandhlawana, Arnold considered it an occasion to carry out "a more speedy extension of the Englishry ... its spread is the spread of future civilisation." He realised other races – especially the Celts whose nationalism he disagreed with – might demur at this. In 'Irish Catholicism and British Liberalism' he wrote that to the English

Ireland "must be an occasion ... from time to time of mortifying thoughts." Later, in *The Incompatibles*, he urged the English to do "perfect justice to Ireland" with a rule more equal and just to the Catholic Irish. John Bright, the Manchester politician, remarked after reading the essay it was strange that Arnold "who could see so clearly in the case of Ireland should run so blind and mad in the case of France." In 1886, after the collapse of Gladstone's Home Rule bill for Ireland, Arnold commented that the plan to "merge Ulster in Celtic Ireland" was a mistake, for "it should be kept distinct as a centre of natural Englishmen and loyalty." Present-day Americans should note that he observed they "are not closely informed on Irish matters".

Arnold's last lecture as Professor of Poetry was given on 26th May 1866 as 'The Celtic Element in English Poetry', and was published as *On The Study of Celtic Literature* in 1867.

The book was a collection of essays, with Arnold's avowed aim of converting middle-class Philistinism, this time by an infusion of "light and emotion" into the practicality and stolidity of English materialism, which he views as "the invention of the Philistines," and by a poetry of "natural magic." In fact Arnold is trying to reconcile his critical intellect with his youthful love of Romanticism, of the unrestrained "caprice" he is determined to reject, by disguising capriciousness as an acceptable because Celtic poetic norm.

He may have been influenced in this stance by the Arts and Crafts Movement, one of whose founders in 1861 was William Morris. Strongly opposed to mass-production – in art as well as industry – it was to become characterised by rich patterns and colours, sinuous lines and floral motifs. The movement grew and became known as Art Nouveau – Gothic art and the paintings of Blake amongst other influences supplying many of its motifs. A predilection for nature, for ornamentation and strong colour put it in opposition to the accepted notion of classical art as pure, plain and symmetrical. Its heyday was in the 1880s and 90s, the paintings of Gustav Klimt and the architecture of Charles Rennie Macintosh and Antonio Gaudí representing its greatest achievements. Languid arabesques of twining vegetal decoration foreshadowed the Minoan art forms discovered on Crete after 1900; much of the appeal of Minoan art was rooted in its similarities to Art Nouveau – and much of the interpretation and reconstruction of Minoan art and architecture (such as Evans' 'reconstitutions' of buildings in Knossos) was based on Art Nouveau theory, as articulated by Ruskin and Morris, forty years previously.

To illustrate his critical approach to what he considered Celtic poetics, Arnold's narrative poem 'St Brendan' of 1859 attempted to reconcile Romanticism (slack formal unity and emotionalism) with the classical criteria of objectivity and control. But, as ever when trying to represent critical theory by poetic practice Arnold, as he himself admitted, failed.

Culture and Anarchy

In 1862 the Newcastle Commission introduced the Revised Code, which in the interests of economy tailored payment to state schools by results achieved. These were the schools of the established church (the Church of England) supported by taxes. But after the Reform Bill of 1867 non-conformists comprised the majority of the electorate. They did not like paying taxes for C of E schools whilst having to support their own privately. Arnold viewed their outlook as "dismal and illiberal," as provincial, that is not of the centre, not actively involved in public life. These were the Philistines. The Populace, as John Dover Wilson says, was an unknown quantity.

The years after 1850 were immensely prosperous and smugness set in, "vulgarity, moral, intellectual and social, preparing to break over us," finding expression in his poem 'Dover Beach', "swept with confused alarms," its last three lines almost summing up the themes of *Culture and Anarchy*. The 1860s had experienced riots such as that in Hyde Park in 1866, which to Arnold and others such as Carlyle smacked of anarchy. He linked these to the spiritual anarchy prevalent in the great industrial cities, to the arrogant growth of personal liberty and divisive forms of Christianity. He believed order could only be secured when the population learned self-discipline through culture "which seeks to do away with classes, to make the best that has been thought and known in the world current everywhere."

Published in 1869 (revised 1875), *Culture and Anarchy* consists of:

Author's Preface
Introduction
1 Sweetness and Light
2 Doing as one Likes

As the *Author's Preface* is an abstract of most of the subjects covered in *Culture and Anarchy* I shall look at it in detail.

"The whole scope of this essay is to recommend culture as the great help out of our present difficulties; culture being a pursuit of our total perfection by means of getting to know ... the best which has been thought and said in the world." This sets the tone for the essay, the definition of culture as "the best which has been thought and said" being reiterated many times throughout, as are two or three other core definitions such as "the study of perfection" and "sweetness and light," a phrase borrowed from Swift. Culture is not something pedantic or futile, and if even an illiterate applies "the best thoughts upon his stock notions and habits, he has got culture." But an Academy, such as that in France, was unlikely to supply these, Arnold considering that it would lack disinterested members. To Arnold, culture is the study of perfection, and true human perfection is harmonious perfection, "developing all sides of our humanity." Non-conformists develop only one side of their humanity becoming "mutilated" as a result: in "*provinciality* they abound, but in what we may call *totality* they fall short" (Arnold's emphases). The smug non-conformists are felt to be out of touch with the main current of national life. "They Hebraise," by which Arnold means they sacrifice all sides of their being to their religious side, leading to a failure of perfection. The established church and the universities favour many-sided development and totality, but "hole-and-corner forms of religion ... inevitably favour provincialism." The establishment or state – and whichever class comprised it – had therefore a definite and necessary role to play in the diffusion of culture.

The ability to read and think is not enough – mass education without higher instruction leads to intellectual mediocrity and lack of general intelligence, and general intelligence is what we lack because "we worshipped our machinery so devoutly." By "machinery" Arnold means our arrogant and hardened attitudes, with a play upon our belief in the superiority of English industrial civilisation and its ensuing smugness over right-thinking. This notion of knee-jerk intellectualism may have been suggested by Swift's *Discourse on the Mechanical Operation of the Spirit*, Newton's mechanical universe and, after 1859, Darwinism with its explanation of life as a mechanism of pre-programmed choices and outcome.

The strongest part of English Philistinism is the "Puritan and Hebraising middle-class, and ... its Hebraising keeps it from culture and totality," Arnold noting that the Americans spring from this class. If non-conformism were to remain unrestrained it would stamp out Hellenism, and "Culture and the harmonious perfection of our whole being, and what we call totality, then become quite secondary matters."

The present discomfort, as Arnold calls it, he sees as arising from the lack of "spirituality, and sweetness and light." The cure to this Puritan narrowness lies not in widening the established church to accommodate their differences (latitudinarianism or Tractarianism) for such a course takes no account "of the course of history, or of the strength of men's feelings in what concerns religion." The answer is to let the Presbyterian (i.e. Puritan) church-discipline "appear in the national church once more" as it had at the Reformation.

Christianity had once been such a narrow sect until Constantine made it the established religion – "or let us rather say, placed the human spirit, whose totalty was endangered, in contact with the main current of human life." This is more important to a man's total spiritual growth, perfecting the gifts given to him, "which is his business on earth," than any speculative opinion he may hold. Culture lets us avoid both Benthamism "or an inadequate conception of the religious side in man," and Miallism "or an inadequate conception of man's totality" that leaves him in holes and corners. Bentham, who died in 1832, had founded Utilitarianism, a moral philosophy that stressed individual freedom and the right to pursue one's own interests without legal restriction; the goal of any law therefore should be the greatest happiness for the greatest number. J.S. Mill had attacked his wilful ignoring of the quality and "poetry" of life. Miall was an anti-establishment non-conformist much despised by Arnold. This stress on individual liberty, as Arnold was to say in chapter V, on doing freely and as we like, has "at the bottom of it the disbelief in right reason as lawful authority."

To achieve perfection culture must be independent of "machinery" such as the shouting belief in the affirmation of the self, and its other rigid forms of self-expression, and make "a quite disinterested choice of the machinery proper to carry us towards sweetness and light." In an assertion still immensely relevant today, Arnold states that a part of machinery's false intelligence lies in calling "the desires of the ordinary self ... edicts of the national mind and laws of human progress." Politicians beware, for we should not mistake "our natural taste for the bathos for a relish for the sublime." We must see things as they really are, and thus it is fatal to the liberals to concentrate on their "liberal nostrums" because they have been flattered into doing so, flattered for their policies "instead of graver social ends" ("loving to hear what gratifies them," he says in *Equality* in *Mixed Essays*, 1879). Instead of looking inward and spirit-curing, liberals look outward to the arena of politics, to machinery of thought and ideal.

Now is the time to Hellenise, "for we have Hebraised too much," yet we must not dismiss the habits and discipline of Hebraism that rescue a man's life "from thraldom to the passing moment and to his bodily senses" (again, of relevance today in the politics of sexuality) for their faith "lies in the substance of things hoped for, the evidence of things not seen."

The *Author's Preface* sums up what the rest of *Culture and Anarchy* expands, analyses and proposes, the intellectual and religious influences of Dr Arnold and Newman being strikingly obvious in parts. Contrary to what the reader may think, the problems raised by Arnold did not die out with the advent of the 20th century but have, if anything, increased in power and urgency, and even now at the start of the 21st century have yet to be resolved: his statement in the *Conclusion* that "we are still engaged in trying to clear and educate ourselves" is as applicable now as then. Nor are these problems concerned solely with religion or aesthetics – the aim is to educate the whole population (by organising all higher education under state control) in how to think disinterestedly. This is to be achieved by studying the 'best that has been known and thought" in both art and science, in order to achieve not only a whole life – a "harmony of perfection" – but a spiritual and social equitability that will triumph over the machinery of our blind impositions upon others.

The six core chapters of the essay allow Arnold to illustrate what occasionally can be rather abstract language (expressed at times in lengthy sentences, many interrupted by a number of sub-clauses that can cause the reader to lose his way) with concrete examples of his theme. Some are amusing in their reference (such as the incident of the Alderman-Colonel of the City Militia who forbade his men to quell the Hyde Park riot in case they sullied their uniforms or lost their rifles), some ironic, some wryly prejudicial.

At times Arnold indulges in linguistic play as, for example, in *whole/hole* where a number of times he conjugates "whole perfection" with "hole-and-corner". He is also partial to neologising, as in the famous 'Barbarians Philistines and Populace' which he carries over from *Essays in Criticism*, definitions based on the cultural characteristics of the upper, middle and lower classes (materialised, vulgarised and brutalised respectively). Often such neologisms are in contrasting alliterative pairs: Miallism as selfish and aggressive individual liberty, Millism as the necessary authority of the state; Hellenism as "spontaneity of consciousness," Hebraism as "strictness of conscience" (his father in disguise perhaps), the distinguishing mark of the Philistine oblivious to the search for truth. Arnold saw the necessity for both in culture (indeed western civilisation has been described as an edifice supported by the two pillars of Hebraic morality and Hellenic intellect). Hellenism is the free roving of the human mind and spirit, Hebraism its Blakean constriction within moral and legal prisons.

Above all, Arnold recognised the inevitability of the 'populace' replacing the middle-class as the ruling class. BBC liberals should note that he saw 'popular' culture as a ploy by the middle classes to manipulate lower class attitudes: "an intellectual food prepared and adapted in the way they think proper for the actual condition of the masses." As has often been pointed out, Arnold himself was not immune to the ideal of imposing middle-class values on popular culture – an ideal also followed by Marxists in the Soviet Union – but by trying disinterestedly to ensure their rightness of thinking and judging, Arnold hoped the working-class would avoid the anarchic tendencies thought to be inherent in popular rule, "because without order there can be no society, and without society there can be no human perfection."

St Paul and Protestantism and *Literature and Dogma*

St Paul and Protestantism was published in May 1870, and was in the long tradition of the composing of sermons more for publication than for parish consumption, occasions for indulging rhetoric and style without the oratory. Fielding satirises such practices in *Joseph Andrews*. Even so such literature was almost as popular with Victorian readers as the novel. In *St Paul and Protestantism* Arnold attacks the dissenters, those who refused to conform to the rules and rituals of the established church, taking the text of "Paul's account of God's proceedings with man, and whether this tallies with the Puritan account." He argued that whereas the dissenters were reactionary, the established church was socially and intellectually progressive. Arnold's aim, in line with his ideas of literary and political standardisation, was a church that could unite all Protestants and eventually accommodate Catholics too. He argued that non-conformism missed Paul's "essential doctrine". This argument is close to the Tractarian position (at Balliol he had preferred going out with the harriers to discussing the great Tractarian issues of the day that so absorbed Clough), and I suspect he was using the Oxford Movement to further his ideology of uniformity.

The Oxford Movement was an Anglican High Church movement that started in Oxford in 1833, advocating traditional forms of worship. The movement's principles were outlined in *Tracts for the Times*, published in Oxford between 1833-41, giving rise to the alternative name of Tractarianism. One of its chief protagonists was John Henry (later Cardinal) Newman, brother of the Francis so excoriated in *On Translating Homer*. Arnold was much influenced by Newman's style and rhetoric though not his beliefs: his poem 'The Voice' (1844) tells how Newman's preaching "blew a thrilling summons to my will/ Yet could not shake it." But Arnold would recognise his intellectual debt to Newman for the rest of his life.

The Oxford Movement began as a defensive response to the spate of reforms in the 1820s and 30s which undermined the established position of the Church of England. The Test Act of 1827 allowed Nonconformists to join governmental bodies; school education in the 1830s was taken partially under government control (and both Oxford and Cambridge Universities became secularised); civil registration broke the Church's monopoly of baptism, marriage and burial; the commutation of tithes freed landowners from supporting the Church. England ceased to be an Anglican state and disestablishment was seen as the logical conclusion (as it became in Wales and Ireland).

At first the movement was launched to defend Church property (when Matthew's godfather John Keble sermonised on "national apostasy" in July 1833), but became more concerned with doctrine. It reasserted the Catholic inheritance of the Church of England, the apostolic succession, the sacraments and the Prayer Book. Its growing spirituality was soon seen to more than replace its lost institutional privileges, and the modern church should note that it could now concentrate on spiritual salvation. But the re-establishment by the Pope of bishops and cathedrals in England raised the question of spiritual authority and became an invitation to Anglican clergy to secede to Catholicism (which Newman did in 1845).

In February 1841 Newman published *Tract 90*, which argued that certain of the Thirty-nine Articles could be seen as supporting Catholicism. Oxford erupted and Newman was forced to resign his Oriel Fellowship. The movement had now affected the whole nation in its moral and spiritual impact. Emotion, especially enthusiasm, became characteristic of the Tractarians (regarded by their opponents as the happy-clappies of their time), coupled with the medievalism so attractive to the Romantics. A new type of piety emerged, close to Catholic feelings, and in the late 1840s even monasticism was revived. Ritualism, a natural counterpart of the revival of Catholic methods of devotion, and medievalism became characteristic of the movement too (anti-Catholic and anti-ritualist riots took place regularly). Though Arnold's wife Flu was a "zealous High Churchwoman of the Tractarian School," as a contemporary described her, 'Stanzas From The Grand Chartreuse' (1867) depicts Arnold's increasing spiritual uncertainty which, assailed by Parnassus and Tractarianism in turn, finally and sadly turned away from the irrelevance of a religion become less spiritual and more ritualistic.

Behind its loss of privileges, however, lay a much more serious problem for the Church. Religion itself had been seriously undermined and the very authority of the Bible questioned. In 1846, D.F. Strauss presented a human Christ stripped of the historical myth. Other German scholars had shown the Bible to be a patchwork of history, legend and nationalistic wishful thinking, and explained Christ's miracles in logical or scientific terms, or even as party tricks. Charles Lyell's *Principles of Geology* (1830-33) refuted the literal meaning of Genesis and pushed history – and creation – back millions of years; Lyell was a great influence on Darwin, who in *The Origin of Species* (1859) had unsuccessfully tried to hide the staggering implication that mankind was not a divine creation but merely the chance product of evolution.

The Church was also seriously weakened by its social bias. The middle and upper classes regarded it as a bastion of social order in a revolutionary age: Disraeli – "moody, black and silent" as Arnold described him – saw Christianity, somewhat cynically, as "the only security for civilisation" in an age of increasing secularism and materialism. The drift of people to the cities had left many rural churches almost empty and many in these new urban classes, especially in the great conurbations where the Church had ignored their needs, felt hostile towards the Church. The Oxford Movement attempted to re-convert these classes by building churches in slum areas, but low attendance remained and still remains.

It is thus not surprising that many had self-doubts about their beliefs: in 1835 Keble told Dr Arnold to squash his doubts by "main force," to cure himself not by reading and controversy but by diet and regimen (Newman's brother Francis wrote of Dr Arnold: "one would think to read him that enquiries into articles, biblical inspiration, etc, etc, were as much the natural functions of man as to eat and copulate"). This forced suppression of self-doubt lay behind the emphasis of Carlyle, Ruskin and Morris on squashing "self-listenings, self-questionings ... diseased self-introspection." The dialogue of mind with itself, as Arnold called it.

By the 1880s the Oxford Movement and the spirit of early Christianity it had tried to recapture, had faded away, but its influence had spread to other fields: *The Ecclesiologist* advocated rebuilding decaying churches in a "thorough and Catholic restoration ... to recover the original scheme of the edifice." If that was impossible then the restored parts, like new churches, should be in the Middle Pointed style. Restorations were to be an act of faith – faith in archaeological findings, and faith in the moral superiority of Middle Pointed. This unfortunately could lead to architects and clergy alike giving churches an appearance in which they believed, not one for which they had incontrovertible proof. As Viollet-le-Duc said: "to restore a building is not to preserve it ... or rebuild it; it is to reinstate it in a condition of completeness which could never have existed at any time." – admirably illustrated by Evans's 'reconstitutions' at Knossos – and the Jorvik Viking Centre.

This early or primitive Christianity attracted Newman but the attendant 'priestcraft' and ritual annoyed Dr Arnold, who wanted the Movement to concentrate on a national church that would accommodate dissenters, instead of wasting its efforts on questions of apostolic succession and ignoring practical Christian morality. His intellectual influence on Matthew, who had characteristically refined it by creating another set of definitions – Miallism and Millism – is obvious in this essay. Edward Miall was a non-conformist who regarded the Establishment as evil; J.S. Mill regarded it as a force for good, and until these two opposite forces had absorbed one another there was no movement forward, Arnold thought, towards perfection. Perfection was a becoming one with God, whom he was to define in *Literature and Dogma* as "that stream of tendency by which all things seek to fulfil the law of their being."

In *Literature and Dogma* (1873), a compilation of previously published essays on biblical interpretation, he argued that Christianity's future lay in laying less stress on miracles and more on intellectual and moral explanation. Without mentioning it, he is of course suggesting a way to refute the implications of Darwinism. The working class, with their increasing education, he saw as rejecting religion altogether. As in *St Paul and Protestantism* he rejected the non-conformist notion of a personal god "as if he were a man in the next street," and stressed the necessity of following Christ's method and "sweet reasonableness" (and thereby aligning the spirituality of Christianity with his philosophy of culture). This method would teach how "he that will lose his life shall save it."

Mixed Essays

In January 1879 *Mixed Essays* was published, marking his return to the theme of national culture. He saw literature (in the preface) as having a social role to play, the helping of humanity to realise itself through society. He reiterated that culture was not for the elite but for the whole of society, and inequality adversely affected all classes, "materialising our upper class, vulgarising our middle class, and brutalising our lower class. And this is to fail in civilisation."

Discourses in America

In 1882 Arnold decided to go on a lecture tour of America. He considered Americans to be more appreciative (and far less rowdy) than the English in their attitude to lectures. He also wanted to pay off his son Dick's heavy debts. In October 1883 he, Flu and daughter Lucy sailed from Liverpool on the first of two lecture-tours of America. He intended (he was unsure about 'Emerson') to lecture on three subjects:

'Numbers; or The Majority and the Remnant', 'Literature and Science' and 'Emerson' concerned the prospects of society in the United States. It may have a huge land area and a large population (the same as Britain's at this time), as Arnold said, but large numbers lack principle and persistence. The majority's judgement is not generally wise and just. But it must not be set aside as ignorant and incapable, only fit to be managed by a property-owning class. The exercise of power by the people tends to educate the people. Even Athens, said Plato, had a very small remnant of honest followers of wisdom. Arnold agrees – Athens fell because the majority were bad and the remnant impotent, standing aside under a wall, as Plato put it.

"The remnant" is Isaiah's term as well as Plato's, and if it was to do nothing the commonwealth of the drunkards and the blind would cause Israel's downfall. But unlike Plato's remnant Isaiah's does not stand aside under a wall in impotence but is exhorted to save the state.

But Judah and Athens were petty states, their numbers too scanty: the remnant has to be relatively large to reform the state otherwise its ideas will transcend the state, not reform it. Modern states have far greater numbers and thus larger remnants, the better to love righteousness and study the law of the Eternal, terms less vague than 'British constitution' or 'American institution.' These moral beliefs are what save states, yet they must accompany one another. Justice must go hand in hand with amiability, and in Ireland the English have begun to give justice but no amiability. Using the popular literature of France as another example, Arnold states that its popularity reflects the unsoundness of the majority, and that this popularity must be withstood, for it forebodes "a most dangerous moral disease".

By implication the majority in America must be unsound too. The Assyrians and Romans had multitude yet neither could produce a sufficing remnant any more than Athens or Judah. Both Britain and America have the advantage of Germanic roots and morality (Arnold was the child of his times here), but America has a greater degree of Puritan discipline, and this gives hope for America to have an incomparable, all-transforming remnant.

'Literature and Science' was given originally as the Rede Lecture at Cambridge in June 1882. It argued that religion and poetry were at the core of humanism, but science also included "the best that had been thought and said in the world" by such men as Galileo, Newton and Darwin. We should study Greek for its more sensitive instinct for beauty, an instinct expressed in terms of classical symmetry: "Fit details strictly combined, in view of a large general result nobly conceived," which he adds can hardly be said of the buildings in the Strand.

'Emerson', a critical essay, is of interest in how Arnold applied his critical standards to a fellow poet and essayist. It opens with his youth in Oxford and the literary influence of Newman, Carlyle, Emerson and Goethe upon his impressionable mind. Emerson to the Americans "was your Newman, your man of soul and genius" with his lofty sentences, but Arnold wishes to search out the "truth about this youthful admiration" of his. How great is Emerson? – quotations from his works have not become current in the English language; he is not a born poet, his poetry according to Milton's strictures is "not simple, not sensuous, not impassioned," lacking plainness and concreteness. His poems have no evolution, being a series of observations. In prose he had no "genius for instinct and style," and like Carlyle he did not know "how to work into a literary composition their materials, and subdue them to the purposes of literary effect." Nor is he a great philosophical writer: he cannot build; his arrangement of philosophical ideas has no progress in it, no evolution." But he is like Marcus Aurelius, not a great writer yet "the friend and aider of those who would live in the spirit," a master of aphorisms, acute observations of life, individualised maxims expressed through a "serene, beautiful temper". His *Essays*, Arnold asserts, are "the most important work done in prose" this century, for he was happy where Carlyle was not, and his conviction that the life of the spirit is happiness suffuses his work.

All three lectures were later published in 1885 as *Discourses in America*, with a short preface concerning the need to educate the familiar Barbarians, Philistines and Populace, and summing up the theme of his lectures in the gnomic statement: "this great law that moral causes govern the standing and the falling of men and nations ... Unless we are transformed we cannot finally stand, and without more light we cannot be transformed."

He hadn't particularly wanted to go, "and I don't like lecturing." He was met in New York by the industrialist and philanthropist Andrew Carnegie, the tour being promoted by Richard D'Oyly Carte of the Savoy Theatre. Arnold's oratorical style was criticised as academical and often inaudible, so he learnt elocution whilst there. As well as New York and Boston, he toured Richmond, Chicago, Ottawa and other cities. He thought the Americans had "freedom from constraint" and did not have the burden of an aristocratic class as did "our middle class at home". He also considered that they were "a parody of the English middle classes, with all their energy, acuteness, self-confidence, narrowness of soul, and vulgarity," a remarkably modern continental view of both countries.

Civilisation in the United States

In January 1888 he started a lecture tour of Hull, Bradford and Bristol, lecturing on his views of America. It was published as *Civilisation in the United States*. Arnold supported its greater democracy, untrammelled by tradition and status, and in this "the Americans have here much the advantage of us". However, he believed their materialism was winning over spiritualism, and their emphasis upon the individual was inimical to the "elevated and beautiful" as he had stated in *Numbers*. He foresaw this would happen in Britain, that society would suffer "the predominance of the common and ignoble, born of the predominance of the average man." This looks forward to our present democratic predicament – how does majority rule accommodate itself to the keeping of "high ideals"?

Essays in Criticism

These were first published in February 1865 as a collection of the lectures and essays he had composed since 1862. The second series was published in 1888 shortly after his death. The Preface sets forth his objectives: "... my efforts are directed to enlarge and complete us by bringing in as much as possible of Greek, Latin, Celtic authors." In other words, to goad English intellectual life into his belief of what constituted cultural perfection. He foresaw a "prosaic practical austerely literal future ... the world will soon be the Philistines." The essays are wide-ranging and cover writers as diverse as Wordsworth and Tolstoy, but the sub-text is that of finding and applying a common ground whereon to rightly judge the value of literature. I choose what I consider the two most important to look at: 'The Function of Criticism at the Present Time' (1865) and 'The Study of Poetry' (1888).

The function of criticism at the present time

In Arnold's view the main critical effort in Europe in art and science has been "to see the object as in itself it really is." But not in England, and thereby our literature was impaired. But, he asks, is creativity not superior to criticism? – for a false criticism may do much damage, but a stupid invention is quite harmless according to Wordsworth. Arnold's answer to this is that a creative mind should also be a critical one. Wordsworth and Goethe both wrote good pieces of criticism. Creative activity is superior to critical activity, but creativity can express itself in criticism and at times should do, for creative activity is not possible all the time and thus a waste of time attempting it.

Creativity, Arnold states, works with the best ideas, "of dealing divinely with these ideas, presenting them in the most effective and attractive combinations, making beautiful works with them, in short." When such ideas are absent great creative epochs in literature become rare. The work of genius is a combination of "the power of the man and the power of the moment," and the power of the moment is best sought by the critic: "both Byron and Goethe had a great productive power, but Goethe's was nourished by a great critical effort providing the true materials for it, and Byron's was not." Romantic poetry was premature in that it "proceeded without having its proper data, without sufficient materials to work with." Wordsworth "should have read more books, among them ... those of Goethe whom he disparaged without reading him."

But it was not lack of reading that lacked to this poetry – Shelley and Coleridge were deeply read where Sophocles and Shakespeare were not. But these latter "lived in a current of ideas in the highest degree animating and nourishing to the creative power". Society was permeated by fresh thought. All the books in the world are only valuable as they are helps to this fresh thought. The widely combined critical effort of Germany formed such an atmosphere for Goethe to thrive in. But he had no national glow of life and thought as was present in Periclean Athens or Elizabethan London. Nor do we have it at present, nor a force of learning and criticism as was found in Goethe's Germany.

Why did such an atmosphere not come out of the French revolution, asks Arnold. The answer, it seems, was that the revolution took a political turn. The Romantics "had their source in a great movement of feeling, not in a great movement of mind". And it was this movement of mind, this intelligence, that marked the French revolution. Where the English revolution asked of a thing: is it practical, is it according to conscience? – the French revolution asked: is it rational? Conscience and legality change with time, but reason is "absolute, unchanging, of universal validity". There is a world of ideas and a world of practice, and neither should be suppressed. But the pragmatic English suspect "the disinterested love of a free play of the mind on all subjects, for its own sake," yet criticism is essentially the exercise of this quality, in order "to know the best that is thought and known in the world."

The danger of the French revolutionaries imposing their ideas on Britain was long past, but Arnold reckons that in England's current "epoch of expansion" – by which he appears to mean a broadening of intellectual as well as imperial outlook – their ideas are slowly filtering through and mingling with our own notions. Our material benefits in time will give us leisure to contemplate and will lead to an appearance of intellectual life; the prosperous Englishman "may begin to remember that he has a mind, and that the mind may be made the source of great pleasure". At the moment only faith can "discern this end to our railways, our business, and our fortune-telling" (fortune-telling is his sarcasm for money-counting).

Flutterings of curiosity appear amongst us, and "it is in these that criticism must look to find its account". And criticism must come first in order to express the fresh ideas, then comes a time of true creative activity. The rule of English criticism must be *disinterestedness* (Arnold's emphasis) by keeping aloof from the "practical view of things" and by following "the law of its own nature, which is to be a free play of the mind on all subjects which it touches". It is to know the best that is known and thought in the world and to make these known so as "to create a current of true and fresh ideas". Its business is not with practical consequences and applications.

The bane of criticism in England, to Arnold, is that practical considerations cling to it. It serves men and parties aiming at practical ends. The *Edinburgh Review* and *Quarterly Review* are merely organs of the Whig and Tory parties, the *Times* of the smug Englishman in general. The *Home and Foreign Review*, Arnold implies, was shut down because its free play of mind served no man or party. Thus British criticism has not kept man from a retarding self-satisfaction, has not made his mind dwell on what is excellent in itself. But does not critical detachment from practical life condemn it to slow and obscure work, he asks. As most people are satisfied with inadequate ideas, and as on these ideas rests the general practice of the world, those who look for truth will find themselves in a tiny minority, and sincerity can only be achieved by arduous and long searching. And who is to say that seen from another perspective our much praised British Constitution is not revealed as "a colossal machine for the manufacture of Philistines."

The critic in England remains exposed to misunderstandings, for the English fail to see that without disinterested treatment of things, truth and the highest culture are out of the question. It happens that in pursuit of truth one can write a book based on a false conception – should we then disparage it, for if a group such as the liberal party or religion seeks perfection should we not applaud it "for their general utility's sake? By no means; but to be perpetually dissatisfied with those works while they perpetually fall short of a high and perfect ideal."

These elementary laws of criticism can never be popular in this country, which is why Arnold feels they must be asserted again and again:

- to maintain independence of the practical spirit and its aims, no matter how important;
- to remain dissatisfied with well-meant efforts if they are impoverished ideally;
- to refuse to be hastened by the demands of practicality;
- to stay flexible and to know when to attach and when to withdraw from things;
- it must study perfection in spheres that may be inimical to the practical sphere, and where the practical finds beneficence it must seek out its spiritual shortcomings, and yet be neutral to both sides. Arnold exhorts us to us enlarge "our stock of true and fresh ideas," but having found one let us not "be running out with it into the street, and trying to make it rule there."

He then asks what subject-matter should literary criticism most seek. This is determined "by the law of its own being ... a disinterested endeavour to learn and propagate the best that is known and thought in the world, and thus to establish a current of fresh and true ideas." As the majority of the world is not of English civilisation this means that much of the best that is known and thought must be foreign. The English literary critic must therefore study foreign literature and seek ever fresh knowledge. Literary judgement should come second to this search for the best, as a guide not as an abstract law-giver. Sometimes with subject-matter fresh knowledge is out of the question and criticism must be all judgement. But the critic should never become abstract but keep a "lively consciousness of the truth of what one is saying". Arnold then places current English literature below that of France or Germany on the grounds that there is less of the 'best that is known and thought in the world' in this country. The critic therefore should know one great literature besides his own. And in this idea of the critic's business the other essays have their origin.

Arnold stresses throughout this essay the importance of learning "the best that is known and thought in the world" and the search for "fresh and true ideas;" Philistines are pilloried, and these notions as we have seen, were to be repeated four years later in *Culture and Anarchy*. But the criteria of criticism that he offers take no account of the differing aesthetics of different civilisations, whether spatially or historically. Thus we find no mention of Arabic, Sanskrit or Chinese literature – or even Hebrew which was readily available to him – and how we should evaluate them, whether in terms of their own criteria or compared to one another. And what are we to make of his lip-service to Celtic literature and its unspoken 'caprice'? His views are very much Eurocentric, though natural for the day, and at times prophetic as when for instance he foresees the rise of pan-European intellectual movements "bound to a joint action and working towards a common result."

The study of poetry

Arnold wrote the introduction to Thomas Ward's anthology, *The English Poets*, in 1879 (published 1880). This introduction was later known as 'The Study of Poetry', and in 1888 appeared at the head of that edition of *Essays in Criticism*.

All our faiths and dogmas dissolve in time, but "for poetry the idea is everything; the rest is illusion, divine illusion ... the strongest part of our religion today is its unconscious poetry." Poetry is worthier than we have thought, it interprets life for us, consoles us, without it "our science will appear incomplete; and most of what now passes with us for religion or philosophy will be replaced by poetry." It provides knowledge where the others give only parade and shadow. Poetry must therefore be of the highest standard. By the laws of poetic truth and beauty it will become a criticism (i.e. an analysis and guide) of life. A poem's excellence should govern our estimation of it, for the historic and personal estimates can be fallacious. To regard it merely as a stage in the course of literary development is to overestimate it. Even the so-called classic poets must be re-evaluated and rated at their proper value. The historian of a poet or poem "is prone to overrate it in proportion to the trouble which it has cost him" – an observation literary specialists would do well to take to heart. Thus there are those who compare Caedmon to Milton; the *Chanson de Roland*, in its alleged union of simplicity with greatness, is called a genuine epic – Arnold applies the touchstone of great Homeric lines to it and finds it distinctly wanting. Such touchstones allow the critic to detect "the presence or absence of high poetic quality". Drawing on Homer, Dante, Shakespeare and Milton he quotes touchstone lines that will of themselves help us "to keep clear and sound our judgements about poetry". Such concrete examples are superior to abstractions when analysing what constitutes great poetry.

Arnold follows Aristotle's dictum that poetry in its subject-matter possesses a superior truth and seriousness than does history, and superiority of diction and movement mark its style. The two superiorities are inseparable and "are in steadfast proportion to one another". If truth and substance are missing so too will be diction and movement, and vice versa.

"So stated, these are dry generalities; their whole force lies in their application." Arnold now intends to apply them to the course of English poetry. He starts with Chaucer. His poetical importance needs no historical estimate, for he is "a genuine source of joy and strength, which is flowing still for us and will flow always." His language, as with that of Burns, is "a difficulty to be unhesitatingly accepted and overcome." How is his poetry superior to French romance-poetry? – in substance, by his large kindly view of humanity, and in style by his "divine fluidity of movement". This liquid diction can be traced through Spenser, Shakespeare, Milton and Keats. But his fluidity of movement was not dependent upon the fluid state of English pronunciation in his time, it was dependent upon his talent.

"But Chaucer is not one of the great classics." Though he transcends all poets for the next two hundred years he lacks "the high and excellent seriousness" of a poet such as Dante, "which gives to our spirits what they can rest upon." But he has "poetic truth of substance ... [with its] exquisite virtue of style and manner."

Because we all recognise Shakespeare and Milton "as our poetical classics" (though I suspect he dared not openly attack their monumentality) Arnold passes over them to the next stage of English poetry, and here, "divergency and difficulty begin". We have an historic estimate but does it coincide with the real estimate – are Dryden and Pope poetical classics? After the Restoration came an age that felt it needed to free itself from its obsession with religion, that it needed a new type of prose to deal with an age of reason and science. Such a prose of necessity brought with it "a touch of frost to the imaginative life of the soul". Its qualities of regularity, uniformity, precision and balance involved "some repression and silencing of poetry". The poetry of Dryden and Pope was such as befitted an age of prose and reason but, asks Arnold, is their application of ideas to life a powerful *poetic* one (his emphasis)? Masters of versification they undoubtedly are, but in comparison with Shakespeare, Milton and Chaucer they reveal themselves as classics of prose not poetry. To Arnold, "Gray is our poetical classic of that literature and age," but his position is singular. He has not the power of poets who have attained to an independent criticism of life, but he was steeped in knowledge of Greek poetry, he "caught their poetic manner" even if it was not self-sprung in himself. "He is the scantiest and frailest of classics in our poetry, but he is a classic."

At the end of the 18th century we start to meet with a huge increase in the personal as opposed to the real estimate of poetry. The real Burns lies in his Scotch poems, not his backward-looking "English" ones. But his world of drink, religion and "Scotch manners" (Arnold's euphemism for country fornication) is not a beautiful one; often it is harsh and sordid. His poetry is unsatisfactory, not because it is bacchanalian but because it lacks sincerity; "we suspect" it is bravado and not the real voice of Burns, that it is "something therefore poetically unsound". Though a man of "vigorous understanding, ... a master of language" powerfully applying ideas to life, that application is not made under the conditions "fixed by the laws of poetic truth and poetic beauty". There is no high seriousness, and high seriousness comes from absolute sincerity. Arnold applies a touchstone line from Dante to illustrate that Burns does not speak to us from the depths of his soul – he preaches to us. The perfect poetic accent is missing. The real estimate of Burns is that his work has truth of matter and truth of manner "but not the accent or the poetic virtue of the highest masters". Arnold much admires "Tam o' Shanter' and the 'Jolly Beggars' as "superb poetic success", and after reading Shelley and his "many-coloured haze of words ... no contact can be wholesomer than the contact with Burns at his archest and soundest."

Arnold hesitates to tread on the "burning ground" of poetry so near to his own times, that of Shelley, Byron and Wordsworth (in a letter to Clough in 1848 he had accused Keats of doing harm to English poetry and being, like Browning, overwhelmed with a "confused multitudinousness"). Most estimates of Romantic poetry he considered "personal with passion" so he ends with Burns, exhorting the reader to apply his method of criticism to gain the benefit of "being able clearly to feel and deeply to enjoy the best, the truly classic in poetry", for though an era of common literature is about to break over us great poetry will never disappear, its future is assured "by the instinct of self-preservation in humanity".

What are we to make of these two important pieces on criticism? Since their publication many critics in various disciplines have devoted themselves to analysing and mostly dismissing his method. They have also stimulated writers into a deeper assessment of their own work: a despairing T.S. Eliot finally declared that only poets should judge poetry. But we should bear in mind that Arnold was attempting to create a method of criticism that was independent of any prejudice, historical, scientific, religious, personal – or educational. It was to be "a self-organizing activity ... it was an art, the act of judgement" as Annan says, "a calling because the quality of life itself must be the concern of the critic". And we should not forget how fond Arnold was of saying "poetry is at bottom a criticism of life." As such the critic was also a moralist, and this attitude lies at the heart of his emphasis on high seriousness. Arnold could thus apply himself to write productively on any and every thing.

His belief that the criticism of a poem is a judgement also of the poet and the value of the culture that gave rise to him, appeals of course to the standards set by the classical Greeks. But the Greeks themselves would not have agreed with his statement that most of what is best and known in the world was to be found, on the grounds of their minority, outside Greece, amongst the despised barbarians of Phoenicia, Egypt, Persia and Babylonia; creativity like power does not depend on its place in the statistical bell-curve. Classical standards by their own constrictions could not encompass romanticism (and its off-shoots, the fantastic, the thriller, the supernatural) let alone its own pastoral romances. The human need for such literature was and is a serious threat to the notion of "high seriousness" as proposed by Arnold. Such standards were ill at ease with the emotional or existential, and openly scornful of any fresh direction in poetry such as symbolic expression or linguistic experimentation. And where is his analysis of the critical standards of that other great epoch of literary creativity he cites, Elizabethan London, a civilisation of medieval Christianity refined by the renaissance and lightly coloured with classicism? The answer may be that criticism does not liberate creativity as he avers, but follows and fossilizes it, and the possibility remains that he suspected this.

Be that as it may, Arnold brought to academic and layman alike an awareness of the importance of criticism and the need to have some standards – besides the prejudice of the personal and the monumentality of the historical – by which to judge art and thereby improve one's own delight in, and appreciation of, the exploration of mind. His appeal to the classical standard as the best standard may not have survived, but his belief in the importance of critical thought, of isolating it from the emotionalism and machinery of politics or religion or economy, from the imperative of practicality, is a necessity in any age. Its aim of furthering the progress of mental perfection is perhaps even more important, even if only to the "remnant" of society who despair of its rush into a tyrannical egalitarianism. And it's still unfulfilled, for we need only to search the academic web to find the dead flies of essays written by critics who appear to have been well educated badly.

4

The Growth of the Pastoral Elegy

I mentioned in my foreword that this essay is structured to culminate in an analysis of 'Thyrsis'. As a poem 'Thyrsis' falls within the pastoral elegy form, though this may not be obvious at first reading. Consequently it is dependant on a long ancestral line of such poetry from Shelley and Milton to Moschus and Theocritus, from Romanticism through Augustinianism to Alexandrian classicism, and can only be fully appreciated if one is conversant with its genealogy. This chapter concerns itself with that genealogy and readers may thus feel it is somewhat digressive. But as Northrop Frye says of the pastoral elegy: "we can get a whole liberal education simply by picking up one conventional poem and following its archetypes as they stretch into the rest of literature" (*Anatomy of Criticism*, 1957). "Whole liberal education" includes exploring the roots of the great majority of English poetry, pastoral as well as other. And this liberal education was an integral part of the tradition Arnold had been steeped in, as we have seen from his *The Function of Criticism at the Present Time* and *The Study of Poetry*, whether classical and philosophical or of the wider arts of medieval England or contemporary continental Europe. With Frye's passionate statement in mind about the importance of the form, I make no excuse therefore for dealing widely, if not deeply, with its origins and its profound influence on English poetry in general and 'Thyrsis' in particular.

The pastoral elegy as Arnold inherited it was the result of the development and eventual integration of three originally distinct elements:

- the ritual elegy
- the Alexandrian pastoral

– Christian exegesis

The core of course was the premature death of a friend and fellow poet.

Over time each of these phases took over the main structural function, incorporating earlier structural features to a greater or lesser degree. At its purest (almost to the point, Robert Graves claimed, of being "strangled by its own art",) the full integration of these three elements and their equal distribution of structural weight may be seen in Milton's 'Lycidas', but there was a long history of experimentation in both form and content before the pastoral elegy took on the shape most familiar to us.

The ritual elegy

Ritual elegy, as the name suggests, is no more than the linking of the religious ceremony, known as ritual lament, to a poetic form called the elegy, and I shall explore each of these in turn.

The ritual lament

Ritual lament – orchestrated public mourning to purge oneself and society of the violent and fearful emotions unleashed by the death of a god, a hero, a loved one – is nothing new to us, and the core of such communal grief is the hope of meeting our dead in the next world. At the grave side we pray for the resurrection of our parents or friends, and to such an end a TV commentator describes in hushed Miltonic tones the burial of a king or a Churchill. The prayer becomes reality – Elvis is seen serving hamburgers in The Rover's Return; Princess Diana becomes a Hindu goddess of love. Cynical or not, we cannot come to terms with our own extinction and – even if in secret – hope for some sort of resurrection for ourselves by piously wishing it for others.

With the advent of city-states in the fourth millennium BC, tribal mourning turned into festivals of public lamentation for the dead king or dying god. The Greeks, in common with their older neighbouring civilisations, had been mourning the annual death (and looking forward to the annual rebirth) of the gods of fertility and vegetation for many centuries, before their Hellenisation of the Near East after Alexander the Great's death in 323 BC speeded up their assimilation of the religious and political systems they had inherited by conquest.

Since neolithic times and the invention of farming (c.10,000 BC in northern Mesopotamia) mankind had been intrigued by the withering of his crops in autumn and their sprouting up again in spring. Burnt by the sun they appeared to die and lie buried in the earth till the spring rains brought them back to life. The seed of such crops, especially staples like wheat and barley, took on a magical aspect: it represented death because the dying stalk dropped it into the earth, and life because from the embracing earth it sprang into life each year. If man killed the corn i.e. harvested it, its death provided him with life in the form of bread, but its death was also waiting to be resurrected as it lay in its earthy grave; the earth by extension became a womb of life, a mother to all vegetation.

There was, then, some force or power in vegetation that defeated death – but why didn't mankind undergo the same transformation after death? The answer appeared to be that vegetal life – and its mother earth in which it was rooted – held some sort of divinity where man's obviously did not. And what if this divinity for some catastrophic reason failed to appear one year, but remained trapped in earth, in the underworld, in death? It became necessary to ward off the unthinkable by yearly appeals to the vegetation god to return to life and thereby renew the earth's fruits. Over time these appeals assumed the form of great ritual festivals where the participants both apologised for killing the god and tried to persuade him to return the following springtime. These rituals often enacted the death of the god in a sort of processional drama through the city; in very early times some went so far even as to dress up a criminal or slave as the god and kill him, not only as the representative of the dying god but also as a scapegoat, a sacrifice to the god to assuage his anger or as a bribe to ensure his return. In later versions the necessary killing of the god at harvest time was felt to be not murder but a freeing of the divine spirit from the physical constraints of the corn (or other crop). Sometimes, to relieve mankind of the guilt and consequences of divine murder, a third party such as another god was blamed for the yearly death of the corn-spirit. Of course the vegetation god may not wish to return to his former constraints, enjoying instead the delights of the afterlife (from which mankind was excluded), and further bribes and rituals became necessary.

At its simplest, the vegetation god was a male who was seduced by an earth goddess (a lady of all life) and either killed or abducted to the underworld, taking with him the powers of earthly regeneration. (In Greece, however, it was Persephone the barley-goddess's daughter who was dragged down to the underworld; and there are hints that prehistorically Ishtar and Isis also played the role of the Dying God.) As a consequence winter drifted over the earth, the corn figs and vines withered, and mankind began to starve. Winter (and its attributes) often took on a divine, usually malignant i.e. anti-human, aspect, and in turn had either to be ritually killed or driven away (the 14th century poem 'Sir Gawayn and the Grene Knyght' provides an interesting variation on this theme). Many scholars have seen in such exorcisms the beginnings of drama: the clash between two powerful forces and the defeat of the one by the moral (pro-human in other words) superiority of the other. Later versions further complicated matters by splitting off certain aspects of the main protagonists and deifying them as lesser or greater players in the eternal drama.

These divine forces were represented in the Sumerian city-states by Damuzi the Shepherd King (Tammuz in Hebrew) and the goddess of procreation, Inanna, better known as Ishtar. Later equivalents of Tammuz, are the Phrygian Attis and the Graeco-Phoenician Adonis. In fact, most of our knowledge of the Sumerian myth has been handed down by Greek writers commenting on the Adonis version of it. Every September, known as 'The Month of the Festival of Tammuz', after the midsummer heat had drunk up life and burnt the fields of Sumer, dirges and lamentations were sung over the effigy of the dead god:

> In Eanna, high and low, there is weeping,
> Wailing for the house of the Lord they raise ...
> The wailing is for the great river; it brings the flood no more.
> The wailing is for the fields of men; the grain grows no more.
> The wailing is for the fish-ponds; the dasahur fish spawn not.
> The wailing is for the corn-break; the fallen stalks grow not.

> All this because:
> The lord shepherd of the fold lives no more
> The husband of the heavenly queen lives no more.
>   (E.O. James, *Comparative Religion*)

The god's effigy was washed, anointed, dressed, painted red and possibly cast into the Euphrates, to take with it to the underworld, where all life it was feared was about to be imprisoned, mankind's pleas for the god's return from the underworld. There Tammuz lies in the sleep of death like a seed of corn lies waiting for rebirth in the earth, and Ishtar herself has taken on his afflictions, diseased and naked, in the dwelling of Irkalla, Lady of Death. Ea, the god of water, persuades Irkalla to release Ishtar by sprinkling her with water; Tammuz is awakened and the lovers return to earth and miraculously:

> The figs grew large; in the plains trees thrived ...
> Where grass was not, there grass is eaten
> Where water was not, water is drunk ...
>   (E.O. James, op.cit.)

So to ensure the return of the lady of all living things her dead lover had to be resurrected and brought back to life, and nature miraculously blooms again. One may care to see here roots of the Grail myth and the young knight's bringing back of fertility to the wasteland.

A similar role in Egypt to that of Ishtar was played by Isis, wife of the life-bringing Osiris, but he was killed and dismembered by his evil brother Set (from the same root as Satan, 'man's adversary') so that life could never again return to the Nile-silted fields. Isis roamed Egypt (part of her journey included Phoenician Byblos), gathering up the scattered remains of her husband and blessing each spot they were buried in. Eventually she restored his mummified remains to life and conceived Horus by him. Osiris is often depicted as ithyphallic, or with wheat sprouting from his chest, symbols of the return of fecundity and sexual potency to drought-stricken Egypt.

An important point to notice for our purposes is that the very early pharaohs were believed to become Osiris at the moment of death and partake of the delights of heaven; the rest of humanity unfortunately had to put up with a wandering ghostly existence for the rest of eternity. At the heb-sed festival the king renewed his youth by enacting his own murder (as Osiris) and journeying into the underworld. At his return to life he would demonstrate his rebirth with feats of running, leaping and bowmanship, and the pyramids may well have been built both to symbolise and theatricise this ritual as well as monumentally framing its reality when the king truly died. Over the millennia this pharaonic privilege was seized by an ever-growing number of his subjects, each hoping to be resurrected as Osiris in the next world, as compensation perhaps for not being able to return to the pleasures of this one. But even this afterworld was not completely independent – the dead lived by the gift of food, wine and prayer from their living descendants, like a tree sustained by the earth it struggles to escape. Once the gifts stopped there was the horrifying possibility of the dead returning to haunt their descendants. Today in some countries mourners still tear their clothes and cover their heads with dust to stop the dead from recognising them.

> Her yellow locks that shone so bright and long,
> As Sunny beames in fairest somers day
> She fiersly tore, and with outragious wrong
> From her red checks the roses rent away.
> (Spenser, *Astrophel: A Pastorall Elegie,* 157-160)

If over the millennia of Egypt's history Osiris and Isis evolved from vegetal to spiritual godhead the same cannot be said of Lityerses who remained – literally – a grim reaper. The supposed son of King Midas of Phrygia, a land-bridge between the civilisations of Assyria and Persia and the Greek colonies on the Anatolian coasts, he would forcefully challenge strangers to a corn-reaping contest on the banks of the Meander, the loser to be killed. As Lityerses was always the winner he would then wrap the stranger in a sheaf of corn, behead him with his sickle, and throw the sheaf and its grisly burden into the river. We may interpret this myth as symbolising the Phrygian's belief that the corn-spirit lived in the ears of grain, retreating before the reapers to the last sheaf. The reaper unfortunate enough to cut this last sheaf was seen to represent the corn-spirit, taken over by the cornered god, and was slain to promote further fecundity, and as a scapegoat for the other reapers. The throwing of the sheaf-wrapped corpse into the river acted as a rain-charm to promote fertility of the fields. In very early times the last reaper was also eaten. Later, to allay the reapers' yearly fear of being slain, the trapped corn-spirit was allowed to escape, but no further than into the person of the first stranger to pass the cornfield. Lityerses finally suffered the fate he meted out to others when the Sicilian shepherd Daphnis (popularly believed to have been the inventor of pastoral poetry), seeking his abducted mistress, found her at Lityerses' court. He was challenged to the corn-reaping contest, but Hercules took his place and killed the king. Lityerses, then, was both the last reaper to whom it fell to kill the corn-god and the divine sacrifice to that god. The early rites of Attis similarly involved the yearly slaying of his priest-king representative, and a survival of such a sacrifice may still be seen in the English Mummers' plays.

Thales, a Milesian of the 6th century BC (Miletus largely controlled trade between Greece and Phrygia), reached the conclusion that nature was life and life was water. The Lityerses myth may have acted as his stimulus – by ignoring the ritualistic and symbolic, Thales was free to speculate on the facts remaining. Such an approach was taken by succeeding Greek philosophers. Poetry however could not cut itself off from its roots of emotion, metaphor and myth – such as did tended to sink under a weight of rationality into a self-righteous austerity, some even into propaganda. Lucretius may still be taught but Ovid lives. Empedocles like Lucretius wrote his philosophy in hexameters: there is both fixity and change everywhere, he said, birth and death being merely rearrangements of one another, an idea that in spiritual terms seems to lie at the heart of the Eleusinian Mysteries. Again we may glimpse here the ritual cycle of the Dying God explained in purely physical terms.

Lityerses was possibly a forerunner of Attis, the Phrygian god of vegetation. Originally he had been a shepherd loved by Cybele, the Great Mother of all living things, but he had betrayed her trust and she drove him insane. Underneath a pine-tree sacred to Cybele he castrated himself and was carried dying to her temple. After he was buried the land became diseased and waste until Cybele brought him back to life. She commanded that in future her priests should castrate themselves in his honour, and on 24th March of each year, 'The Day of Blood', they would carry an effigy of Attis on a bier of pinewood, marching through the streets to the sounds of cymbals and flutes (which Cybele had invented), recalling the mourning of their goddess for Attis, ecstatically slashing off their testicles amid streams of blood (in early Christian times popes had to prove they were not pagan by showing intact testicles). On the following day her worshippers celebrated the return to life of Attis. Taking place at the time of the spring equinox this festival of Cybele and Attis was seen as the rebirth of nature in springtime.

Like Attis to the pine tree, the early English god Woden hung to an ash tree (as were human sacrifices to him) and both were ritually stabbed. The similarities with Christ's death are obvious, and Old English literature's obsession with the image of Christ nailed to the cross make us suspect that they were really worshipping Woden, the god of the hanged. Whatever the truth the ease with which the English absorbed foreign beliefs and ideas made the transition from pagan myth to Christian – and later classical – imagery that much easier.

With the death of Alexander the Great, decades of internecine wars erupted as his Macedonian generals fought one another for mastery of the empire. After the battle of Ipsus in 301 BC the empire was divided between the survivors. Ptolemy added Palestine and Lower Syria (Phoenicia) to his Egyptian kingdom, and it was at this point that the cross-fertilisation between Hellenicism and the Near Eastern civilisations began to blossom.

The Phoenician god of vegetation was Adonis and, in common with the other Dying Gods described above, there were numerous variations of his myth with their ensuing contradictions. Originally an eternally flowering tree-spirit, he was killed by castration (represented by a wild boar) and taken down to the halls of death. On the spot where he died the red-and-white (blood and dead flesh) anemone sprung up. Drought and famine swallowed up the earth until his lover Aphrodite begged Persephone, Lady of the Underworld, to release him for four months every year so that beasts could procreate and nature thrive. With the spring rains the river Cydnus ran red with earth as if with Adonis's blood down to Byblos, fertilising the land; women would carry the effigy of Adonis as if for burial and throw it into the sea. The god was drowned but rose again the next day. The red waters of the Cydnus thus united the bloody death and life-giving rebirth of Adonis at a single point in time. An interesting commentary on this processional ritual, seen from the aging Aphrodite's point of view, is Yeats's poem 'Her Vision in the Wood', where Adonis – *that beast-torn wreck* – is doomed to an eternally youthful cycle of death and rebirth, unable to recognise his eternally aging lover beyond his self-perpetuating world. In Eliot's *The Waste*

Land Aphrodite has followed a similar path, becoming Tiresias the emasculated prophet, ever present but doomed to an all-knowing ineffectiveness. In the twentieth century, it seems, rebirth has bloated itself out of hope into that eternal horror forever slumbering in our subconscious, and the pastoral elegy has ironically become the medium of nihilism.

Because death and rebirth were united at one point in time, as with the other Dying Gods, Adonis's festival could be celebrated either at his death in late summer or at the spring equinox of his rebirth in late March when we celebrate Easter (Christians changed the name anemone to Easter flower), for previous times and modern accountants the start of the new year. In Byblos and Alexandria this festival was held in late summer. Worshippers would prepare a marriage-bed, surrounded by the fruits of summer, cakes of honey and pastries baked in the shapes of animals, flowers blossoming in pots – the 'gardens of Adonis' that may have characterised the Hanging Gardens of Babylon and which still hang outside some London pubs in deference to the spirit of the barley – for the yearly remarriage of Adonis and Aphrodite. Around their bed the people would sing songs of sexual encouragement. The flowers, miniature gardens, fenced with silver pales as Theocritus describes them in his 'Idyll 15', like the god, would soon fade and die:

> Soon, Aphrodite, comes your joy's eclipse!
> At dawn, before the dew fades from the ground,
> Your lover must be carried out and drowned:
> We'll float him seaward, singing our lament
> With loosened hair, breasts bared and garments rent.
> Half-god, half-man! Adonis, you alone
> Cross back to this world over Acheron.
> (Trans. Robert Wells *Theocritus – The Idylls*)

Next day the marriage-bed had become his bier, and amidst wails and sorrowing it was carried out to sea where Adonis sank in a splash of flowers to his watery grave.

> Goodbye, Adonis. I pray that you find us here,
> Healthy and happy, when you come back next year.
> (Robert Wells, op.cit.)

It was this eternal human longing for health and happiness in this world that both linked and added to the various myths of the Dying God: what to some was an irrational means of perpetuating food production was to others a form of sympathetic magic, whereby the spirit if not the body of the fertility god could be born again in the life-giving corn and seen stretched at ease in a field of anemones or golden daffodils. And if to the Greeks it seemed an alien god like Adonis could provide shelter against want it made sense to incorporate it into their pantheon, a back-up to Demeter the barley goddess, Persephone her daughter and Hades king of the dead. Perhaps our welfare state is no more than Tammuz without the divinity – and the pastorals to celebrate it.

The elegy

Outbursts of weeping and the passions of grief assume a natural rhythm of both movement and speech that in primitive tribal mourning took on poetic form. From the evidence of palaeolithic cave paintings and other anthropological studies it appears that at the dawn of history appeals to the Dying God to return consisted of the dance – leaping and thumping, stamping mother earth (as English morris dancers still do with their sticks), shouting at her to release her child of spring – and perhaps these thumps and shouts in unison gave rise to the rhythmical units of poetry (the metric term feet may reflect these primitive beginnings – the Greek word spondee derives from a phrase meaning something like 'drunk-foot'). The old man in 'The Pardoner's Tale' thumps the earth for opposite effect – *Leeve mooder, leet me in!* (445) an Eleusinian reminder that death is necessary for rebirth. Elegy, "a song of lament especially for the dead ... a poem in elegiac metre", as the *Concise Oxford Dictionary* defines the term, comes from the Greek elegos, a mournful poem. It referred to a specific verse form (couplets consisting of a hexameter, the favourite Greek metre, followed by a pentameter line) and to the emotions frequently conveyed by that verse form. Any poem in this distinct form was known as an elegy, irrespective of subject-matter.

Though in English the pure elegy, i.e. a distinct and recognisable literary form, is unknown, there were at least two early attempts to institute such a form by means of stanzaic refrains. The Old English poem *Deor* (c.870) with its melancholic refrain at the end of each stanza – *Þaes ofereode; þisses swa maeg* – and *Pearl* (c.1380) with its 20 variated sectional refrains. In general almost any structure and metre can be used to support the elegiac theme, from the solemn rhythm of the requiem mass to a jaunty lyric, and one only has to compare Tennyson's 'Ode on the Death of the Duke of Wellington' to Whitman's 'When Lilacs Last in the Dooryard Bloomed' to see the few points of contact, or contrast 'The Boke of the Duchesse' to Dunbar's 'Lament for the Makaris' to see the disparity. Elegiac passages in other verse forms did of course occur in Greek, as for example the deaths of Patroclus and Hector in the *Iliad*; but these passages are not free-standing elegies but prosodically and thematically part of the epic, as is the death of Enkidu in the Sumerian *Epic of Gilgamesh*, or Beowulf's burial, though often they must have been recited out of context.

The important festivals of the ancient world had as their climax recitations from the great religious myths. These recitations used elevated language, a stateliness of tone, and a prosody – or at least a paratactic device such as repetition – that tried to encompass the differing emotional rhythms of the plot. Everyone participated in these sacred dramas as an act of faith – the notion of an artistic or aesthetic pleasure to be taken from such participation would have been not only profane but unintelligible: art had not yet freed itself from religion and we should remember this when reading those pieces of ancient liturgy that deal with the Dying God, for no amount of intellectual pleasure on our part will substitute for ritual participation in it.

The Eleusinian Mysteries in honour of Demeter's search for her daughter, Persephone, who whilst gathering flowers was stolen suddenly into winter and death, was open to everyone who considered themselves to be Greek. For such a great festival it is remarkable that so little information about its procedures and meaning has come down to us. Demeter, as Apuleius tells us, was a Mother Goddess worshipped under many names in many lands: Cybele to the Phrygians, Athena to the Athenians, Aphrodite to the Cypriots, Ishtar (Inanna) to the Akkadians and Sumerians, but, as he says in *Metamorphoses XIa* "the Egyptians called her by her right name, the queen Isis". It seems, though we cannot be sure, that the Eleusinian Mysteries stressed life from death, Persephone from Hades, the dormant corn-seed from the cold dead earth (the Greeks stored their grain-seed in underground chambers), and by extension the immortality of the soul. The myth was poeticised in the 7th century BC 'Hymn to Demeter', though the poem is in no way elegiac nor does it concentrate on the participants' emotions (grief, awe and hope).

The mysteries were Apollonian i.e. there was an appeal to a rationality and a spiritual if hidden meaning within the ceremonies: the religious orgies on the other hand were Dionysian, frenzied with wild music and wilder dances on midnight mountains where the votaries, wearing horns on their heads and draped with snakes, tore to pieces a bull or a calf (or even a man in the case of Pentheus) to achieve a mystical union with eternity. A group partaking in a common emotion externalises it; thus projected it becomes the god they experience: we close our eyes in holy dread at the visionary in 'Kubla Khan' because he has achieved synthesis between man and god. The frantic rhythms of such bacchanalia took form as the dithyramb, a wild choral hymn or dance, and the dithyramb according to Aristotle gave rise to tragedy.

In the sense that it bolstered and propagated the political supremacy of priesthood or kingship the Lityerses myth never became a state ritual. But it did provide Greek peasants with eternal themes for their reaping songs in short lyrical form – "one of the early plaintive strains of Greek popular poetry," as Arnold describes it. Allied to such forms were the Linus (or Ai Lanu) and Maneros reaping songs, named after the refrains in the various ethnic songs the Greeks heard as their culture spread throughout the Near East.

The Maneros song

As soon as the first sheaf was cut Egyptian reapers sang out *Maa ne hra*, "come to the house," because the corn-spirit was believed to live and die in the first sheaf cut, and by being offered a place of refuge his return the next year was assured. The Greeks heard this pronounced as *maneros* and assumed it to be the name of the son of the first Egyptian king, Menes, as they assumed Lityerses to be the son of King Midas.

The Linus song

In Phoenicia and Syria a similar song was sung by reapers at vintage and harvest time. Linus or Ailinus was thought to be a shepherd, torn apart by his own dogs, and possibly representing an intermediate stage between Tammuz and Adonis. *Ai Lanu*, ran the refrain, "woe is us".

The Lityerses song

At threshing and reaping time in Phrygia the corresponding song of joy and woe was the Lityerses Song, sung before the last sheaf was cut. As we shall see, it took many forms.

So what in terms of the elegy have ancient rituals and dirges given to the form? If Cicero's definition of the mysteries is correct, whereby its initiates "have not only received the method of living with joy, but also of dying with better hope," then we can see here the emotional dynamism that characterises elegy – a dynamism that applies to mourned and mourner alike. An emotional if not formal structure is in place, the potentiality of a form built on platforms of ascending passions (grief, bewilderment, angry contemplation, self-help), that culminates in hope for both the grieving and the dead (Hopkins's 'The Wreck of The Deutschland' explores this potentiality with the minimum of support from other elegiac props). This letting-down of the hair, ironically to Arnold the critic we might erroneously think, owed more to Dionysian influence than to his oft-quoted Parnassian ideals of Apollonian rationality and austere aestheticism. To the pastoral as a literary form the answer is more concrete: ritual and dirge supplied the themes of nature in physical and symbolic shape, and it's to the pastoral that I shall now turn.

The Alexandrian pastoral

The growth of the pastoral in 3rd century BC Alexandria, the centre of the Greek world after the death of Alexander the Great, as a new literary form seems to have been a reaction to the nullifying supremacy of earlier Classical literature such as the epic, lyric and drama. Alexandria was a city intensely aware of itself, of its relationship to the past and present Greek world, of its precariousness on the edge of a vastly ancient Egypt: it was perhaps no accident that the great library founded by Ptolemy I concerned itself with cataloguing and defining the Greek achievement as a phenomenon both different and superior to anything previously experienced.

In general the pastoral's main features were:

- a singing match or poetic contest (in Greek terms one was much the same as the other) between two contestants
- the narrator's use of dialect, poetic or otherwise
- the use of images drawn from nature
- the description of common-or-garden objects
- a natural setting (a field, a spring, a farm) and its flora and fauna
- the appearance of, or appeal to, local nymphs and lesser deities
- the lowly life of the contestants (shepherds, goatherds, milkmaids)
- the introduction under various personae of the author or his friends
- bawdiness of dialogue
- a resolution in the form of a prize, or a decision to move on to another activity

Shepherds and goatherds were preferred to reapers or ploughboys because the latter were felt to have the harder and therefore less noble, or at least less apt, jobs; there were times of idleness for the shepherd in which to dally and play the pipes, and of course the shepherd could trace the pedigree of his labour back to Tammuz, Daphnis, Linus and Attis – and to the poet-shepherd Hesiod.

The form such poetry takes is known as the idyll, a short descriptive poem of a picturesque scene or incident, especially in rustic life. Compact and polished, it appears to have been developed – if not invented, with respect to Daphnis – by Theocritus, a Sicilian-born poet who flourished c.270 BC under the patronage of King Ptolemy II in Alexandria, though he himself did not use the term. Strictly such poetry should be called bucolic; later grammarians however referred to the form as the idyll (or in the case of Vergil, the eclogue). 'Pastoral' is a convenient, if somewhat capacious, term under which to group such literary forms.

A good example of how the pastoral worked is Theocritus' 'Idyll 5', a singing contest between a goatherd and a shepherd, to be adjudicated by Morson the woodman. There are strong dramatic features to this idyll – the loathing of the contestants for one another, barely prevented from breaking out into fisticuffs by their challenging one another to what is little more than a flyting match, the tension being finally resolved by the award of a lamb to the goatherd. The references are homely and natural, occasionally directed to the gods of local springs and groves, and the bursts of idiomatic or bawdy dialogue remind us how rooted in the humdrum reality of his world Theocritus was. But the dramatic action of the idyll carries no moral judgement in its resolution, and may even be ironic in its use of a woodman to replace the *deus ex machina* of Euripidean drama: the fact that the catamitic shepherd lost out to his onetime sodomiser is due to his lesser abilities as a poet, not to the reprehensibility of his past sexual actions.

Where a small group of people find themselves isolated for long periods, like shepherds in high summer pastures, social and sexual conventions tend to lose their restraining power. This homosexuality (and even bestiality) in the Alexandrian pastoral was to become a problem of moral concern to audiences of our own civilisation; as Gabriel Harvey wrote in his notes to the January eclogue of Spenser's 'Shepheardes Calender':

> In thys place seemeth to be some savour of disorderly love, which the learned call paederastie: but it is gathered beside his (Spenser's) meaning. For who that hath red Plato his dialogue ... may easily perceive that such love is muche to be alowed and liked of ... to be praeferred before gynerastice, that is the love which enflameth men with lust toward woman kind. But yet let no man thinke, that herein I stand with Lucian or hys develish disciple Unico Aretino in defence of execrable and horrible sinnes of forbidden and unlawful fleshlinesse.

However, buggery (the word refers to the practices of Bulgar monks) had an ancient pedigree amongst the English upper classes even by Elizabethan times, perpetuated by a peculiarly English educational system. Since the time of St Dunstan and the monastic reforms of the 10th century, the upper classes had been sending their sons to be educated as far away as possible from the moral influence of the family, whether as scholars in the great cathedral-schools or as squires in a distant relative's castle, and during the late eighteenth century they began to send them to public schools. By Dr Arnold's time, as Murray notes, many of these schools had become sinks of buggery, inflamed by drunkenness, bullying, fagging and mass floggings. Savage if not sexual rites of passage (also common in the Lancashire cotton mills), riots, gross illiteracy, heavy gambling, locking up of masters in their own rooms and a general terrorising of the countryside (prompting his description of the aristocracy as 'barbarians') were seen as the natural order of things. These depravities, partly portrayed for example in *Tom Brown's Schooldays* by Arnold's Rugby friend Thomas Hughes, Dr Arnold was determined to eradicate when he was appointed headmaster of Rugby school in 1828.

So the unfortunate Hobbinol in Spenser's January eclogue – however much Harvey may try to gloss it with Classical excuse – was to be the first and last shepherd in the English pastoral tradition to attempt to seduce with *His clownish giftes... His kiddes, his cracknelles, and his early fruit* a fellow shepherd. Pastoral buggery tried to disguise itself as transvestism – *As You Like It* being but one example – but even this ploy did not escape the execration of Puritan critics such as William Crashaw, until the 'enormitie' of buggery, no matter how poetic, was hurled headlong from the English hedgerow.

Theocritus himself spoke and wrote the Doric Greek of Syracuse, a city founded by Corinthian colonists around 700 BC, even when he was living in highly sophisticated Alexandria, and seems to have been proud of it if Praxinoa's retort (in *Idyll 15, The Festival Of Adonis*) to the accusation that she spoke with flattened vowels is indicative of his attitude:

> We come of good Corinthian stock, the same as
> Bellerophon. We're women from Syracuse, famous
> For our quick tongues, and we're proud of how we speak.
> Who dares say we Dorians don't talk proper Greek?
> (Robert Wells, op.cit.)

There was literary precedent for the use of dialect in Greek poetry. Over time a convention had grown up whereby certain poetic forms became associated with certain dialects: drama with Attic (but choruses in Doric), lyric with Aeolic, and epic a curious mixture of Aeolic and Homeric phrases strapped to the back of Ionic. Doric – save for Arcadian which it almost surrounded, Arcadia being a thickly wooded mountainous land whose inhabitants spoke a form of the Mycenaean 'Linear B' that Achilles and Agamemnon possibly used – was the dialect of the Peloponnese, and its colonial form was used by the school of Pythagoras for the writing of philosophy. There appears to have been no social stigma attached to the use of dialects, though that didn't stop Aristophanes from satirising the more outlandish of them as a source of laughter or Theocritus from using them as a means of characterisation; Spenser uses archaisms and 'country' speech in 'The Shepheardes Calender' as proof of literary pedigree; T.S. Eliot – acting the deconstructionist in that monumental parody of the pastoral elegy, *The Waste Land* – uses dialect to support the theme of cultural degeneracy.

Theocritus' successors in the use of pastoral were Bion and Moschus; after them some of its elements grew top-heavy and broke away to become known as the pastoral romance, characterised by less realism, ornater language (usually in prose), a thin plot crammed with a great deal of action enacted, often in disguise, by characters and specifically lovers of a higher class. These undergo numerous adventures – still in the pastoral setting – before a marital resolution is reached. This sub-species degenerated into atrophy throughout the late Hellenistic and Roman periods but was stimulated by medieval interest in the didactive narrative poem (Chaucer's 'The Knyghtes Tale' for instance), and eventually became incorporated into Elizabethan drama, both comically (*A Midsummer Night's Dream*, Fletcher's *The Faithful Shepherdess*) and pseudo-tragically (*The Winter's Tale*, *Pericles*), persisting through the lavishness of Jonsonian masque to Milton's *Comus*.

The beginnings of the pastoral elegy

The Epic of Gilgamesh was a collection of ancient Sumerian sagas about a mythical king of Uruk, collated, edited and translated into Akkadian around 1200 BC by one Sin-liqe-unninni, a warlock from Uruk, who fashioned them into the standard epic we know today. Tablet VIII of this version (recovered from Nineveh and now in the

British Museum with the rest of the eleven tablets) describes Gilgamesh's lament for his dead friend Enkidu, the Wild Man, and shows remarkable similarities to some of the distinguishing characteristics of the form later known as the pastoral elegy:

The procession of mourners

Amongst the mourners listed are all the beasts of the wild, the sheep pastures, the Euphrates and Ulay rivers, the cypress and cedar, the young men and elders of Uruk, the ploughmen and shepherds, the brewer, the harlot who civilised Enkidu and other courtesans of the court and temple (these latter were to take the leading role as mourners in elegiac literature, representing the common human experience of death). Fresh in its day, such all-inclusive lists of mourners were to become the conventional stock-in-trade of the later pastoral elegy. What draws it closer to the elegiac form is its inclusion of the urban as well as the natural world; but unlike the list of mourners in a conventional pastoral elegy the list is not exploited in any obvious referential way, such as thematic use as symbolism of death and rebirth, but it does link Enkidu's death to the renewal of crops and thus to the city whose life depended on a fat river and yearly agricultural surplus.

Flower and water imagery

The water imagery is strong – the sacred river Ulay in Elam and the pure Euphrates represent the life-blood of nature – and in Tablet IX Gilgamesh reciprocates to the (beneficial?) judgement on Enkidu by stating his intention to dam the Euphrates, presumably to irrigate the dead land after spring rain. Afterlife for Enkidu ensures new life for Uruk, and brings to mind the Lityersean sacrificial stranger (Enkidu's having been brought by guile to Uruk from the plains of Sumer makes us suspect that originally he had been chosen as a divine sacrifice).

Reference to flowers or their universal symbolism is noticeably absent and may suggest that in a sophisticated society such as Uruk's the ritual of the Dying God was more concerned with the physical return of summer crops than with the imagined return of the spirit within them.

Nature imagery was often used as a recitative sympathetic magic to bring back new life into what was dead. But no use is made of this function in *The Epic of Gilgamesh*, the poet preferring to use nature imagery as a general appeal to the whole world to mourn; the function of sympathetic magic is expressed instead through his reference to worldly treasures. Gilgamesh ransacked his treasury for gold, copper, alabaster, cedar, ivory and carnelian to provide the grave goods that would enrich Enkidu in his afterlife and ensure he wasn't doomed to an eternity of dreariness and hunger; unfortunately the only artifacts we can recognise are a copper breast-plate and a death-mask of lapis lazuli as the tablet is irreparably damaged at this point – an archaeologist's pickaxe appears to have gone right through the middle of it. Sacrifice to the gods of the underworld of fattened oxen and sheep is followed by a description of rich, marvellously wrought artifacts to be offered by the dead Enkidu as gifts to the underworld gods. Sacrifice provided food for the gods, gifts bestowed status and power on them – themes that do not survive even residually in the later pastoral elegy, though it may be that the bestowing of gifts was replaced over time by the strewing of flowers that fulfilled the same symbolic function.

This particular section (VIII ll.134-188) stands alone, with Ishtar and her lover Tammuz framing between them Erishkegal, Lady of Death, and her ghostly stewards. Each god is given a specific gift – presumably symbolic – which Gilgamesh first displays to the Sun God for seeming approval. Structurally this is the core of the lament, an iconographic scene redolent to its audience of some rich and deeper meaning long lost to us. These sumptuous gifts are described in great but often lacuna'd detail, and if truly consigned to the grave would have impoverished the whole city-state of Uruk. However, in the light of Woolley's excavations at Ur in 1927 and the treasures he discovered in its Royal Death-pits with their mass human sacrifice and 'fattened oxen', we should not be too hasty in judging how far our ancestors would go to honour their dead and bribe their deities to bestow everlasting mercy on the favoured. Economy was not then a god.

The narrator's self-pity and bitterness

Enkidu lay dead and Gilgamesh began to mourn his friend ... his curly [hair] he tore out in clumps ... "like a hired mourner-woman I shall bitterly wail". (A. George, *The Epic of Gilgamesh*, London 1999). The power of Tablet VIII comes from its switch to first person narration – suddenly and dramatically Gilgamesh's grief becomes personalised, with its raging impotence in the face of death, its desperate hanging on to the memory of Enkidu's friendship. As in the pastoral elegy this anger results from the tension between the fact of death and the uncertain hope of rebirth. In Tablet IX Gilgamesh bitterly realises that Enkidu's death is a prophecy of his own doom and he goes in search of immortality.

The resolution

The judgement of Enkidu by the gods reverts to third person narration. We are left in ignorance of this judgement, and of the last stage of Enkidu's burial, for once again the pickaxe has been at work, but the judgement was probably that he should be granted an afterlife of bliss. Enkidu is now described first in emblematic then anthropomorphic terms: the axe at Gilgamesh's side, his shield and festive garment, wild ass on the run, panther of the wild who, if not reborn in this world will at least walk with the gods in a glorious afterlife. In this respect he becomes the Dying God, a something more than a worm in a dead nostril or the imagined embodiment of mourners' memories: he becomes the hope of rebirth for both nature and ourselves, even if like Proteus or Gwydion he has to take ever-changing forms to express it.

How much of this lament is taken from genuine ritual, how much is poetic hyperbole? The original Sumerian version of the lament is missing as are relevant ritual texts (though we do have a dark and intriguing poem on the death of Gilgamesh with its reference to human sacrifice that seems to support Woolley's theory about the Royal Death-pits), but undoubtedly the ritual would have been raised in status as well as reinvigorated by being included – and heroically expanded – in what was the first truly international epic. Various parts and versions of it were recopied many times down to at least the 2nd century BC, by which time the Babylonian scribes were speaking Greek as their mother-tongue. The more popular parts were translated into other languages including Hittite – the cultural intermediary between Mycenae and Mesopotamia – and a version has been found in Canaan, whose later name of Palestine derives from the Philistines, refugees from the burning palaces of Mycenae and Crete.

Such was the epic's cultural influence on the Levant that easily in its train came the Tammuz/Adonis and Tammuz/Attis myths. Thus some of the elements of the later elegiac form were already in place from the transmission of the epic or could be easily assimilated because of the epic's international reputation, but constituting only the most basic themes – the outward procession of mourners and their burial gifts (our age is reduced to the collection-plate) and, more importantly, the inner processions of the fear of death and our desperate attempts to defeat it.

The *Iliad* follows a similar scheme when Achilles hears of the death of Patroclus – his rage, the mourners led by his mother Thestis, the first person narration and Achilles' realisation of his own impending death. But crucially he is not scared, he knows and accepts the prophecy that he will die young, thus the scene loses any self-contained tension and has no iconographic force whatsoever. But then this was not Homer's intention – Achilles' anger had to be aroused not against death but against Hector; in this way the epic's action could be speeded towards its resolution: Achilles' reconciliation with Agamemnon, the fight against Hector and by implication the fall of Troy. Whether the *Gilgamesh* had any influence on the *Iliad* is outside the scope of this essay but we can postulate that the death of Enkidu, unlike that of Patroclus, held a thematic and dramatic power that grew over the millennia to fulfil its own ritual and be reborn in Theocritus.

After the Median sack of Nineveh in 612 BC the full version of the epic remained buried under the tells of Assyria until Austen Layard's pickaxe revealed it to the world in 1853. It was not translated (and published in *The Daily Telegraph)* until 1872, six years after 'Thyrsis' had been written. I would like to think Arnold read it (though he disliked that newspaper) and perhaps wondered wryly at the ancient psychology he had inherited in his own imagery.

Of importance to the growth of the pastoral as elegy are those elegiac passages in Theocritus' idylls that Bion and Moschus developed. In particular 'Idyll 1 – The Passion of Daphnis', a lament for the herdsman Daphnis as he lay dying. The gods ineffectually try to stave off death ("Love drags me into the darkness where no songs sound"), strangely reminiscent of the Sumerian vision of the afterlife, "Where clay is their meat ... they dwell in darkness ... on door and lock dust has settled", as was sung at the Festival of Tammuz and by Enkidu on his death-bed. The lament for Daphnis is sung by the shepherd Thyrsis, and recounts the dying herdsman's words to the various grievers around him, wolves and cattle, Hermes, shepherds, the ithyphallic Priapus and others. Already we can see the links between nature, sex and death, but the hope of mortal man's resurrection – and its link to the natural world – is lacking. The link in fact was already in place, but as yet unused, as we have seen in the myths of the vegetation gods – the yearly rebirth of nature, the blossoming and procreation of life after winter death. The reaping of the divine life-giving corn in autumn is accompanied by songs of grief, apology and hope – the Lityerses Song – and in 'Idyll 10 – The Reapers' Theocritus ends the contest between two reapers with such a song, though one that begs Demeter for a good harvest and then pragmatically advocates hard work to achieve it. The vital connection that links mortal man to god, nature and earthly rebirth has not yet shown itself.

Though much influenced by him, Bion tried to vary the pastoral tradition he had inherited from Theocritus. His 'Lament for Adonis' was an elegy (written about 150BC) concerning the young god of vegetation whose impending death, as we have seen, was about to bring impotence, famine and misery to the world: "now that he is dead let them die too, let every flower die". Where Theocritus' 'Festival of Adonis (Idyll XV)' concentrates on the wedding of Aphrodite and Adonis, Bion's poem concentrates on Adonis' death. The two poems may be said to be complimentary parts of the festival, but they are not reproductions of it and were not sung as part of it – they are aesthetic as opposed to religious solutions to the problem of human mortality.

Structurally, Bion's lament is built around aspects of the grief of Aphrodite separated by a variable phrase that acts as a thematic if rudimentary refrain: "Woe for Adonis (or Cytherea), the beauteous Adonis is dead", which may have suggested the "O, weep for Adonais

– he is dead!"of Shelley's elegy. Adonis cannot be reborn until Aphrodite admits he is dead and lets him descend into Hades, for his death – as is made explicit – is also her death. The two are bound to die, they are bound to the cycle of death and rebirth and she must wail again and weep again, "come another year". At this point comes the extended hymn to Persephone, not only the central symbol of life, death and rebirth but the bestower of such regeneration on others.

Bion emphasises the red,white and purple of body and blood, applicable to Aphrodite as well as Adonis, for during her lamention in the wild woods her flesh is torn by briers. She unbraids her tresses and goes wandering distraught, unkempt, unslippered, a phrase which both looks back to the diseased and naked Ishtar searching the underworld for Tammuz and forward to Alexandrian ritual (and Spenser's 'Astrophel'). This inclusive pendulum movement that Bion uses to illustrate the cycle of death and rebirth can also be seen in the ancient giving of burial gifts, Gilgamesh-like, and forward to the strewing the corpse with flowers and perfumes. Yet grief may be assuaged, for "Of the blood comes the rose, and of the tears the windflower" (the windflower is the anemone).

The mourners are the basic elements of nature: the woods and rivers and hills, flowers and fountains, showing the ancient link between the death of Adonis and the onslaught of winter's infertility. Humanity is not referred to, there is no association of Adonis with mortal death nor is the hand of hope stretched out to us, for Bion is dealing with that mythical world before the creation of man when the gods walked the earth, and he thus introduces what was to become a vital ingredient of both the pastoral and the pastoral elegy – the notion of the Golden Age.

Moschus was a friend of Bion; on the latter's death – apparently murder by poison – he wrote his 'Lament for Bion', suggested by Bion's 'Lament for Adonis' and using Theocritus' 'The Passion of Daphnis' (Idyll I) as its structural exemplar. We may say that at this point began the tradition of the pastoral elegy by associating the untimely death of a poet with Adonis and his yearly rebirth in spring, using the ritual imagery of the god's life, death and resurrection. The poem thus marks the start of the connection between mortal man and earthly rebirth.

The elegy comprises thirteen hexameter verse-paragraphs of irregular length separated by a refrain that is distinct and invariable where Bion's is not: "A song of woe, of woe, Sicilian Muses." An analysis of these verse-paragraphs and their arrangement reveals the basis on which future pastoral elegies were to build, though it should be borne in mind that such an analysis hardly does justice to the poem's many qualities.

1   Invocation to nature to weep for Bion. Moschus inverts Bion's lines:
    "Of the blood comes the rose, and of the tears the windflower" with "Pray roses, now be your redness sorrow, and yours sorrow, windflowers." This is the starting-point, that grief is not to be assuaged; as we later read, Bion's spirit may return but his person never will.

2-3 Invocation to the birds of mourning to lament.

4   Bion as herder and Doric Orpheus.

5   Apollo and Pan (musical harmony and poetic ecstasy), the nymphs, the Satyrs and Priapus mourn him. In these last two there may be a biographical reference to Bion's sensuality. Bion is now directly associated with Adonis and the death of nature:
    "For sorrow that you are lost the trees have cast their fruit on the ground, and all the flowers are withered away. The flocks have given none of their good milk, and the hives none of their honey; for the honey is perished in the comb of grief, seeing the honey of bees is no longer to be gathered now that the honey of yours is done away."

6-7 The birds shall never sing so mournful a song again.

8-9 Pan and Galatea weep for Bion.

10 The Loves – Aphrodite's handmaidens – weep for Bion (in the 'Lament for Adonis' they act much more as choric mourners), and Aphrodite is said to love Bion more than Adonis. The river Meles (near Smyrna where Bion and Homer were born) is filled with lamentation. Bion is compared with Homer, the one singing of war the other of Pan: "he both fashioned pipes and milked the gentle kine; he taught the lore of kisses ... and stirred the passion of Aphrodite."

11 "Both town and country mourn for Bion" (as they did for Enkidu): "Ascra makes far louder moan than for her Hesiod, the woods of Boeotia long not so for Alcaeus … Thou leftest others thy wealth but me thy song."

Moschus, like Milton and Arnold, becomes the inheritor.

12 Flowers are reborn every year yet man sleeps a sleep that is without end or waking.

13 Bion was poisoned and song went cold and still. If Moschus could have gone down into Hades like Orpheus he would have charmed Persephone with his songs of her beloved Sicily until, relenting, "she shall give my Bion back unto the hills." As in the 'Lament for Adonis' the extended reference to Persephone acts as the ceremonial core of the elegy, both the end of life and its rebirth being within her gift.

From this analysis we can grasp those elements that later poets were to make into the formal basis of the pastoral elegy (the numbers refer to the verse paragraphs):

Invocation 1, (and the refrain throughout)
Poetic Ability – 2, 3, 8, 10
Poet as Adonis – 5, 10, 13
Presence of Narrator – 11, 13
Biographic – 5? 13
Herders – 5, 10
Mourners (throughout):

Songsters	–	birds especially those associated with tragedy, the nightingale and swan;
	–	Gods and nymphs of song, Apollo, Pan, Cyclops, Galatea, Orpheus;
	–	the Sicilian Muses of the refrain;
	–	the poets Homer, Hesiod, Alcaeus and others;
Nature	–	as in Bion, the flowers, rivers (such as the Meles), springs, woods;
Towns	–	Ascra and others.

Chief Mourner – Aphrodite and her attendant Loves, as in the 'Lament for Adonis'.

The Golden Age – the action of the poem is set four or five hundred years before Moschus' own time, during the imagined clearness and simplicity of early classical Greece, when the herder's life and the citizen's were not in conflict, a golden time before the advent of cosmopolitan corruption and tyranny (Bion was probably murdered on government orders). This scene is not localised but by implication covers Graeca Magna from Sicily to Smyrna.

Apotheosis (the narrator's consolation) – 12, 13. In 12 there is no hope of earthly rebirth, yet if like Bion we can all emulate Adonis (as all Egyptians came eventually to emulate Pharoah and become Osiris) then, as in 13, perhaps a part of us unknown to this reality may live on as a spirit joying in nature's bounty.

I suspect (for example, from Moschus' wondering what song Bion sings in Hades) that both laments have allusions to the Eleusinian mysteries and the nature of human rebirth in another form. This hint or even hope of the unseen resurrection was eventually to be taken over by Christianity, as indeed it took over so many other religious aspects of the Near East – its worship of the divine family, for instance, imitated the Phoenician custom in which each city worshipped a divine trinity, comprising father, mother and son. Whether any significance should be attached to the fact that structurally the poem comprises thirteen sections (ritual coven, the yearly cycle of lunar months and so on), I leave to the reader.

As Highet says in *The Classical Tradition*, "Autobiography takes a nobler turn in the pastoral elegy." From now on poets mourn the premature death of their friends, and to emphasise the youth and freshness of the dead depict them in a wild woodland setting "lamented by shepherds, huntsmen and nature spirits," some of them the poet and his friends in disguise.

This is not to say the pastoral did not continue to develop or have other contributions to make to the elegy. With the defeat of Cleopatra and Antony at Actium in 31BC the known world came under the sway of Rome. But Roman culture was heavily indebted to Greece, some would say to the point of smothering – even its early cultural advances including its alphabet had originated in Greece through the medium of Etruscan. Throughout the Hellenistic period Latin had taken to Greek drama and philosophy, and with the collapse of Ptolemaic power the lyric and the pastoral took their turn and moved to Rome.

Vergil (Virgil is the medieval spelling) and Horace wrote what we call bucolic poetry, i.e. poetry of the countryside that stressed the simpler virtues against the vanity, greed and corruption of Rome the imperial city. The Alexandrian pastoral may have contained the seeds of such a theme but never tended them to maturity. It is here that we can say Horace wrote bucolics and Vergil eclogues, if we wish to specialise the terms which in general are held to be interchangeable with idyll: the bucolic is the life of ease in country retirement, eclogue is the country life transferred to a new land, that other important ingredient of the conventional pastoral, the idealised landscape. To the Golden Age of Bion Vergil added the Golden Land of Arcadia.

The Vergilian notion of Arcadia brought to the pastoral an idealised world of eternal youth. The Golden Age of time is now located in an earthly but idealised world where the god Pan presides over nymphs, flocks of sheep and the spontaneous music of the pan-pipes. Like Priapus the god of orchards, Pan was a follower of Dionysus, the frenzied god of the woods and hills, of the unrestrained outpourings of the poetic soul, and Arcadia was a fitting setting. Pausanias had described the real Arcadia in Greece as harsh and mountainous with strange beings such as werewolves (possibly an echo of the horned and ecstatic votaries of Dionysus, himself a Dying God, but of the vine, or of goat-footed Pan driving herds to the high summer pastures), and ancient and often barbarous customs, including human sacrifice. Such folk-memories may hark back to Mycenaean times – one of the last Linear B tablets from Nestor's palace at Pylos lists ten victims for sacrifice against imminent danger – and after the collapse of their civilisation in about 1100 BC those who had not escaped abroad fled here, managing to defend their traditions and dialect against the onslaught of the Dorians as a dark age fell upon the Aegean. Onto this barbarity – or perhaps it would be better to call it an isolated culture shrunk into degeneracy – Vergil grafted the sense of youthful play, love in idleness, self-expressionism, a dalliance in eternity before the constraints of maturity bend them and us to the pragmatics of this world; before Apollo, the conventional god of music and poetry, imposes as James says his rule of harmony through the sophisticated means of the lyre. Above all, Arcadia was the final escape from the city, its cynicism, filth, selfishness and overcrowding.

But the dark hint of death was also present in Arcadia. Youth was not eternal and the city could not be ignored. To the young, death may be a distant country, but with growing maturity hints of mortality loom ever larger. Poussin the painter was haunted by this revelation that death too is in Arcadia: he painted at least two versions of *Et in Arcadia Ego*, based on an earlier painting by Barbieri that showed two Arcadian shepherds inspecting a tomb crowned with a rat-gnawed skull. Youth, like Adonis, must die.

The pastoral and pastoral elegy as such lay ignored throughout medieval times, pastoral romance being the preferred form. The popularity of the pastoral revived with Sannazaro's 'Arcadia', written before 1481, a mixture of verse and prose concerning a lover who flees to Arcadia. It was based on Boccaccio's 'Ameto' and made heavy use of Homer, Theocritus and Vergil. His work had tremendous influence throughout Europe, and his canzone form was to provide Milton with one of the main structural elements for 'Lycidas'. In English, Arcadia and the pastoral first surfaced in Sir Philip Sydney's 'The Countess of Pembroke's Arcadia', again influenced by Sannazaro especially in the use of metric variation.

Metric variation within the pastoral and its derivatives was little used in classical times. Vergil kept to the 6-foot hexameter and Sannazaro preferred it to other metres. It is a rhythm that is not comfortable in English as it ends each line with two thumps, though it can be used for comic or satirical effect, as for example in Clough's 'The Bothie'. In 'The Shepheardes Calender' Spenser uses 13 different verse forms, and in the collection of elegies for Sydney published in 1595 'The Mourning Muse of Thestylis' is written in hexameters; Spenser's own elegy to Sydney is in 5-footers (pentameters) and he describes it as "a pastorall elegie", with all the formal implications of such a statement. 'Astrophel' is, then, the first example of the form in English.

Christian exegesis

Vergil was made an honorary Christian by the early church because of his so-called 'messianic' eclogue, 'Bucolics IV', that celebrates the birth of a divine child who will bring back the Golden Age. This honorary status and his poetic standing ensured his survival (Dante made him his guide in the *Divine Comedy*) through medieval times to the renaissance. In his 'Idyll 7' Theocritus introduces Lycidas and Simichidas, friends in disguise (indeed, the whole poem may be autobiographical), and this inclusion of one's acquaintances was taken up by Vergil. His enemies Baevius and Maevius appear in the eclogues, and this personal element, with its hints of satire against people or beliefs the author was unsympathetic towards, developed in the renaissance into criticism against the Church. The impact of Christianity on the pastoral elegy was therefore twofold – religious and political.

The religious impact of Christianity

Christ and the metaphors of his parables were easily merged into the pastoral convention – Jesus called himself a shepherd, clergymen are known as pastors (from the Latin for shepherd) leading their flocks, the bishop carries a shepherd's crook and so on, the convention being authorised poetically by 'The Song of Solomon' with its pastoral imagery and love-making. Christ now joined Attis, Tammuz and the poet's persona as a fellow shepherd. "Except a corn of wheat fall into the ground and die, it abideth alone: but if it die, it bringeth forth much fruit" says Jesus (*John* 12, 24) in an Eleusinian aside, and so thematically the rebirth of the Dying God could be linked that much more easily to Christ's ascension into heaven and to the Church's promise that we should all rise from our graves at the Second Coming. The cyclical year was stretched into the cycle of eternity. The yearly resurrection of the Dying God was now seen as a pre-Christian error, a pathetic fallacy as Ruskin termed it in *Modern Painters*, "a falseness in all our impressions of external things," the comforting error of looking into the natural world to reflect our ideas. But as we shall see, this fallacy of Adonis was to sit quite happily with the hope of Christian resurrection.

If Adonis and the other Dying Gods were false prophets, if they were not reborn every spring, why were they not replaced artistically by the true and only God – Christ on the cross? The answer appears to lie in the images associated with the Dying God. At the festivals and in the poetry of his death the imagery of rebirth was particularly concrete, almost joyous, in its references to flowering youth, lambs and kids, the buds and blossoms of the greenwood, the yellow stalks of corn sprouting life below hillsides thick with birdsong, rain on the parched earth, sparkling streams, tears and wailing and happiness. The impression of reborn life was both reassuring and overwhelming. But such images are not associated with the dying Christ. The central image is the dead tree – the cross – and the central figure hanging from it is not reborn at the intervention of mankind; there is no attempt even at intervention. The emphasis is on death, and the reassuring element of resurrection – which balanced classical and ancient ritual – is lacking: here there are no flowers in bloom, no women rejoicing, no god leaping down from his tree, just starkness and a bleak finality. (Christ's rising from the dead after three days appears to be an intrusive hand-out to nature-worshippers.) The happiness has been reduced to a future hope, life after death to a distant promise. A ritual of reality has given way to an act of faith.

Beowulf, the Old English epic of a Swedish warrior, was composed around 650AD and written down about a hundred years later. Beowulf himself dies a hero's death, is burnt and his remains buried under a mound. He goes to Waelhalla (better known by the Norse term Valhalla, the Hall of the Slaughtered) where he no longer partakes in human affairs and where the living cannot reach him nor wish to. His life and death offer no link to the cycle of nature. But at the start of the epic we do have a reference to the early English corn-god Scef, 'sheaf' (of corn), whose descendants included Beow (possibly the original John Barleycorn celebrated by Burns), Angul the eponymous ancestor of the English, and king Alfred. Scef had been put to sea as a child alone in a boat (like Sargon of Akkad and Moses), lying on a sheaf of corn in a shield. Iconographically this may represent the arrival of the spring rains and warming sun that encourage the growth of the young spirit of the corn. Scef may have been the son of Nerthus, the Earth Mother, described by Tacitus as being particularly admired by the Anglii (the continental English) and whose slaves were drowned after ceremoniously washing her, leaving to us bog-bodies to ponder over:

> ... who were in sloughs interr'd alive;
> And round them still the wattled hurdles hung,
> Wherewith they stamped them down, and trod them deep,
>   ('Balder Dead', II 172-4)

Christianity made desperate attempts to drive these English fertility gods underground but they had a nasty habit of reappearing in various guises: pagan rituals resurfaced in 10th century poetry as bowdlerised charms against evil; wood-elves shapeshifted themselves into the mysterious vanishing maidens of 13th and 14th century lyrics; both Wild Eadric – the Shropshire equivalent of Hereward the Wake – and Thomas the Rhymer experienced otherworldly contact with the deadly queens of Elfland. The church could not fully shake off paganism's hold even on itself, as unwittingly revealed for example in the chronicle of Abingdon Abbey, where in the early 10th century to settle a riparian land dispute, the monks floated a shield with a sheaf of corn in it down the Thames so that its god-directed course might mark out the abbey's original meadow boundaries. But *Beowulf* itself with its archaic and classical use of language and outdated references lost its influence in the face of 11th century preference for prose, hagiography and oriental stories; by 1200 it had disappeared from both popular and literary consciousness.

The 8th century poem 'The Dream of the Rood' attempts to expand the paucity of Christian imagery by a splitting of the austere images into their opposites: the cross is both throne and rack, heaven a thane's hall of earthly plenty, Christ is slain English hero and everlasting God. The kennings and oral formulas of Old English heroic poetry have been skilfully manipulated to suit a Christian context. A peculiar slant is given to the poem by making the cross the narrator, a living tree-spirit and a guilt-ridden artefact confessing to the dreaming poet. We are asked to forget this world by suffering with Christ and looking forward to our own death: we could not be further from the spirit of the ancient rituals.

Early medieval lyricists made use of what is known as the Marian lament, a debate between Christ on the cross and his mother, to alleviate this poverty of associated imagery, a leap of the imagination into the historically unattested. *Pearl* uses this debate form within the structure of the dream poem, but between father and dead daughter, to give us relief from sorrow with a vision at its end of the heavenly city. Christian imagery, though used, is outshone by the poet's exploration of the physical and spiritual connotations of the pearl and other gems, as iconographic as the Gilgamesh poet's description of the burial gifts for the gods. The *Pearl* poet (he may also have written 'Sir Gawayn and the Grene Knyght') also introduces what appears to be a classical use of flower and water imagery, but in this he was certainly influenced by the 'New Testament' ("For uch gresse mot grow of graynes dede," says the poet in imitation of *John* 12, 24 above) and the love lyrics of the time, especially as his dead daughter is described as a bride of Christ. This is a powerful and intricately wrought poem, but its use of remote dialect and literary archaisms greatly lessened its capacity to influence later elegists.

The austerity of Christian imagery was rejected by late medieval and early renaissance poets. Christ's resurrection – and thereby ours – provided the thematic core, but the imagery of death was classical, tempered only by local circumstances. The dream was a favourite structural device of the middle ages (it gave an impression of objective truth): in a vision Chaucer sees a knight in a wood mourning his dead wife, but for all its accretions of allegory and references to the Ovidian Arcadia, 'The Boke of the Duchesse' is more of a eulogy than an elegy, sympathetic commiseration with little consolation, the resolution being worked out through mixed references to Christian exegesis and the ideals of courtly love. But the imagery of the greenwood in springtime and Ovid's nymphs and shepherds was to influence later poets long after the dream framework had been discredited. Christian salvation and classical imagery were growing ever closer to one another.

The political impact of Christianity

For centuries up to 1500 the Church had been growing ever more powerful. For younger sons with no hope of inheritance and the clever poor it offered – like the Communist Party in the old Soviet Union – the only means of advancement. To others of an idler nature, joining it provided security against hunger and drudgery, as joining the charity industry does today. Top-heavy with careerists, corruption and highhandedness, it dictated events in this world and praised or damned you in the next. Its economic and spiritual power was boggling. Kings, earls, burghers, churls and thralls alike felt its heavy hand; whole countries like King John's England could be placed under a papal interdict, and by 1530 the Church controlled a third of England's economy (one has only to visit Winchester cathedral to be staggered by the proof of this). And the more wealth it obtained the more its repute sank.

Criticism was muted at first but slowly gained in strength; secure in its position the Church only reacted if it felt doctrine was under attack. Satire blossomed into the swingeing onslaughts of Chaucer and Dunbar. Both Skelton (a suspended priest) and Spenser wrote anti-prelatical satires using the persona of Colin Clout. But it was the hypocrisy that came under fire from these poets – the attacks on doctrine were left to the theologists and so-called heretics were dealt with severely, from Wycliffe to Luther. With the Protestant breakaway the problem of doctrine became acute throughout Elizabeth's reign: should there be an established church, what its rituals and denomination if any, in what language, what about the political rights of dissenters, are bishops needed, does anything come between a man and God – or even, as in the classical sense, between a man and his personal God – except the Bible? Three hundred years later the Oxford Movement of the 1830s tried to re-address some of these problems in the light of current social and political trends (Arnold's father and friends were caught up in its arguments; Clough resigned his fellowship at Oriel College because he could not subscribe to the Thirty-nine Articles), and even today the Protestant Act of Settlement is a sensitive issue. Once a church became the established state religion any criticism of it was interpreted as an attack on the government; and now that Protestant governments represented the heavenly order on earth instead of Catholicism, such attacks were regarded as a treacherous subversion of the natural order, anti-human and therefore by definition satanic.

Political or social commentary in the great English pastoral elegies ranges from the disguised and general to the openly specific. Often, to avoid attention from the authorities, the conventional imagery of the pastoral had a secondary function of being used to imply criticism of the status quo. In 'Astrophel' we are asked:

> What needeth peril to be sought abroad,
> Since round about vs, it doth make aboad?
> (89-90)

Is this an observation of the world, a political crisis, a threat to his own life that Spenser's referring to here? What is the meaning –

seemingly referring to the two-edged sword in *Revelation* 1,16 – of Milton's enigmatic threat in 'Lycidas':

> But that two-handed engine at the door
> Stands ready to smite once, and smite no more.
>
> (130-131)

The only hint lies in the poem's description wherein "the Author ... foretells the ruin of our corrupted Clergy," and in 1637 such a political stance stood almost on the scaffold. Using conventional pastoral imagery Shelley describes himself in 'Adonais', as if foreseeing his own death in terms of Keats', as "A herd-abandoned deer" struck by the hunter's dart, a bitter attack upon literary orthodoxy and its malice's wish-fulfilment in murder that also alludes to the death of Bion. Or Arnold's sly dig in 'Thyrsis' at Clough's poetry:

> ... his piping took a troubled sound
> Of storms that rage outside our happy ground;
> He could not wait their passing, he is dead!
>
> (48-50)

which is also a comment on what Arnold saw as the sterile intellectual arguments of Victorian Britain. Eliot's vision in *The Waste Land* was even bleaker – western civilisation was murdering its own soul in an orgy of reversed values:

> You who were with me in the ships at Mylae!
> That corpse you planted last year in your garden,
> Has it begun to sprout? Will it bloom this year?
>
> (I, 70-72)

Here is death with no hope at all of resurrection, expressed in the conventions of pastoral elegy that sting with irony – the form that expresses hope from suffering is turned in on itself to express suffering without hope.

As the reader will have noticed from the above examples, criticism slowly fell away from the church and aimed itself at the social values of the time. In one sense every time Adonis died a part of our own world died with him, forcing us to reassess both our own lives and the impact others have upon it:

> Thus do we weep and waile, and wear our eies,
> Mourning in others, our owne miseries.
>
> (Spenser, 'Astrophel', 95-6)

In the pastoral elegy the narrator has to come to terms not only with the death of his friend but with his own doubts and values, and finally with his own death too.

In this it was influenced by Renaissance humanism with its belief that man was at the centre of the universe with God at its source. The deity could thus be approached by experiencing, literally or imaginatively, everything it had created until finally one experienced God himself. Humanists believed this experience could best be achieved through 'high magic' not rationalism, though ironically 'high magic' such as alchemy was to lay the foundations of the 'rational' 17th century scientific revolution. The influence of magic on the arts was considerable, thanks mainly to Ficino's translation of the *Hermetica*, a magical tract written down in 3rd century Alexandria that combined the spiritual truths and rituals of the Greek Hermes and the Egyptian Thoth under the name of Hermes Trismegistus in an attempt to counter Greek rationality. Neoplatonism and Jewish cabbalism rapidly attached themselves to it and hermetic method – at least to poets and philosophers – was seen as the most intellectually satisfying way of uniting with God. To these gnostic beliefs came the poet Sannazaro; Vitruvius with his famous hermeticism (in all its senses) of the human body that so influenced the painting of Da Vinci; Botticelli made visual its lore in his *The Three Graces*; Palladio applied it to architectural theory, building by harmonic proportions and numbers equivalent to the harmonies found in the music of the period. The proportions of his Villa Rotunda were built into the design of Lord Burlington's Chiswick House, an attempt to put in stone that which is most pleasing to the eye. Indeed one may postulate that such harmonies underlie the structure of Pope's longer poems.

Hermeticism spread: Paracelsus, Faust and Queen Elizabeth's Astrologer-Royal, John Dee, being among the north's more famous or infamous students of its theory and practice. Spenser applied its numeric symbolism to 'Epithalamium', where the counting of its 'long' lines (365) and stanzas (24 of varying length) and other encrypted numbers reveals the poem's structural basis. In its stately movement through a single day that paradoxically completes the yearly cycle the marriage-song thematises the "eterne in mutabilitie," whereby through procreation we partake in the cyclical harmony of eternity. Hermeticism spawned secret societies such as the Rosy Cross and Freemasonry, wherein 17th and 18th century scientists including Newton found spiritual refuge from the horror of their own discoveries, or the 19th century Golden Dawn which so influenced Yeats with its ritual and mystic psychology. Today its philosophical and artistic influence has waned, leaving a rubble of collapsed lore for Gaeans doomsters and pyramidiots to build newfound Atlantises from.

The humanistic belief that God was the source of the universe took a severe battering from Darwinism. Mankind, bereft of the old certainties of traditional morality and unable to find a new touchstone to differentiate between good and evil, was now seen as moving from its centre into the void left by God; a progress, as Nietzsche described it in 'Thus Spoke Zarathustra' and 'Beyond Good and Evil', through self-transcendence and the will to power – over oneself as well as others – towards man as the sole measure of the universe, the Superman. Human perfection is thus the transformation of man into god, no matter how many dead, diseased children litter his way, for if we define evolution as nature's drive for perfection then of necessity anything imperfect must be discarded. There is no compassion in evolution and if we believe in it our only attitude to the pangs and losses of this world is one of stoicism if not insensibility. If God had not created man then man owed him no responsibility, and in the train of Nietzschean godlessness came the desperate urge to find wherein lay man's responsibility for his own actions, from Marxism, Freudianism and Existentialism to Kafka and *The Waste Land*.

The characteristics of the pastoral elegy

We have seen what the basic elements of the pastoral were, but how have these been applied to the elegy? If we freeze the growth of the pastoral elegy at a particular moment – say at the time of the 'Lament for Bion', where we may now regard it as a distinct literary form –

we find the characteristics that dictate its eventual blossoming (with variations) in English literature to comprise:

- an invocation to the muses
- the Golden Age
- the dead man as a youthful friend and fellow poet (with friends disguised as shepherds)
- the dead man's persona is that of the Dying God
- the procession of mourners who refuse to admit their loss (the 'pathetic fallacy')
- flower and water imagery
- the narrator's self-pity and bitterness
- the resolution (the narrator's apotheosis)

The tension lies between the objective fact of death and the subjective fear of one's own. This tension was structured by the dead Adonis on the one hand, on the other by the renewal of nature and the hope of his return to this earth. The natural imagery of winter and spring acts as a balance between them, as does the narrator's grief both for his friend's death and his own future, the resolution lying in the cancellation of tension by the calm realisation that death may be final in this world but is merely the beginning of eternity for ourselves and our loved ones in the next. The elaborate form of the pastoral elegy is thus used by poetry to control and transcend raw emotion by ritualizing it. And with its drift towards a philosophic emphasis on the ritual theme we can perhaps see here the lasting appeal of the pastoral elegy: an attempt to explore the meaning of one's life and its place in eternity. It is a journey into poetic reality, where "the crude and naked sorrow is veiled and chastened," as Swinburne says, "with soft shadows of the land that is very far off."

5

'Thyrsis' – The God in the Machine

Arthur Hugh Clough, born 1st January 1819, colleague of Arnold at Rugby, close friend and inspirer at Oxford, rival poet in later life, wanderer and critic, died in Florence on the 13th November 1861 and was buried in its Protestant cemetery. In this he followed a tradition other than that of the pastoral – that of the English Romantic poet dying in Italy. 'Thyrsis', Arnold's elegy for his dead friend, was not published until April 1866, simultaneously by *Macmillan's Magazine* and the *Atlantic Monthly*, for £25. "It will not be popular" said Arnold.

Possibly he thought this because 'Thyrsis' is not an obvious pastoral elegy, for where are the mourners, where even the dead Adonis? Is the poem no more than a cold excuse of a pastoral on which Arnold floated his intellectual disenchantment? Dead rituals are not credible in a mechanical age, and Arnold therefore has had to hide (and thus escape the predictability of) the conventional form under an assemblage of acceptable Victorian imagery that had its basis in the Wordsworthian approach to nature, at once floral, anti-urban and philosophical. As these were already present in the pastoral elegy, but only as symbols of, or comments on, the ritual theme, Arnold has had to reverse their function from signifier to what is signified – from symbol to meaning – while still allowing them to stand as symbols. This was not easy to do, especially in an age that questioned the very foundations of art, but the fact remains that Arnold succeeded (he is, after all, the master of understatement): the cuckoo is not only itself, not only the symbol of spring's rebirth but is the rebirth; Lityerses is not just the representation of late summer's death but is the dying god himself. And this duality we must bear in mind when making the journey into the poem's lasting appeal.

Of course the poem is much more than a lament for a dead friend ("not enough is said about Clough in it," wrote Arnold in 1868, and was concerned enough at this not to send a copy to Mrs Clough) – as in 'Lycidas' the narrator keeps personal grief at a distance and thereby objectifies the meaning of death and its relevance to the narrator. As others have remarked, Clough's death is much more the occasion of the poem than its theme.

The plot comprises a triple movement:

– the journey from Oxford to the (unreached) signal-elm
– the journey from evening into night
– the journey from winter into summer.

There are various associative links between these three plotlines – the journey from permanence into change and decay, the growth into maturity of Clough and Arnold, the sentimental journey, circularity of phrase and reference, the journey beyond youth to the golden time of the scholar-gypsy – which help merge and at other times parallel the worlds of Graeco-Hellenism and Victorian Britain. But importantly the physical journey is never completed, and by extension the journey as symbolic cycle of death and life is never completed; and so there can be no parallel interpretation of these metaphoric journeys as obvious thematic symbols – Oxford can represent the contemplative Sicilian countryside as well as the industrial din of Manchester; the night is both death and the dawn of truth; the flowers of summer "And all the marvel of the golden skies" are blasted by "storms that rage outside our happy ground." In short the poem is a complex mixture of pastoral symbolism and the allegory of a melancholic philosophy.

The major theme is the death of the Classical ideal, of its supposed intellectual certainties and warm unchangingness, one of the reasons why the elegy is formatted in English terms. The now impotent Classical gods had once a life whose vitality is depicted against the sterility of British intellectualism; the death of the Classical ideal is the death of English spirituality and Clough has retreated to a world that, though dead, held a golden promise that the Victorian city and its Manchester schools of thought have smothered. But Arnold does not express one civilisation in terms of another as does Eliot – he puts both points of view and finds each equally failing (though he knows which he'd rather live in). The balance between the Classical and the Victorian, between Lityerses and Manchester, is pivoted on the Berkshire countryside – personified in the figure of the Scholar-Gypsy – the tension between the two being resolved in the very last stanza. For this resolution asks the inevitable question arising from the failure of one's lifelong beliefs or expectations: what is the truth of our existence? And truth is what the unreached elm signifies through our search for it.

Between the plot that provides the groundwork of the poem and the theme that gives it meaning is the structure that shapes it. The form this takes is, of course, that of the pastoral elegy, and the best way to see how this form elucidates the theme is to explore its constituent parts in terms not only of the poem itself but of Arnold's intellectual pursuits, beliefs and experiences.

The invocation to the muses

Milton invokes the Sisters of the Sacred Well, Shelley invokes the sad Hour (the Horae were linked to the seasons), as muses to inspire their elegies but Arnold describes his poem as a monody, a song sung by a single actor in a Greek tragedy, thereby signalling that he speaks from a self-contained world of private grief directly to his audience, with the emphasis on loneliness and tragedy. Arnold is doubly alone (Clough was both friend and poet), and the resolution is the voice of Clough reminding him to persist in their quest of "the light we sought" (238), a sentiment followed by Tennyson in 'Merlin and the Gleam':

> – After it, follow it
> Follow the Gleam.
> (IX, 11-12)

This statement of the theme is repeated when Arnold invokes his own unpublished work 'Lucretius', whose burden is that all our actions, all change, all weariness find themselves in the still peace of God. I can see no other reason for invoking his own unpublished work than as a summoning forth of the muse within himself. For this is not invocation so much as evocation, and Arnold not so much invokes external muses as evokes his poetic self, his inner thoughts, feelings and grief and past experiences to provide the inspiration.

His external muses are only indirectly invoked – "ye hills of Cumnor," or Clough's unseen presence, the living ghost in Arnold's memory, and always in the background is the eternal spirit of the scholar-gypsy – for as we have noted, the conventional invocation to classical muses is barely credible in a cynical age:

> ... O easy access to the hearer's grace
> When Dorian shepherds sang to Proserpine.
>   (91-2)

This indirect invocation – the plea to nature to express his self-inspiration – is granted in the descriptions of it throughout the poem and thus brings a concreteness to Arnold's invoking. The conventional and classical is transformed into something new, familiar yet fresh, and acts as a continuous feedback to increase the power of his inspiration.

In most pastoral elegies the muses are invoked within the first stanza or verse paragraph, and these opening lines also set out the metrical basis of the poem. Almost without exception classical elegists used the hexameter as their conventional prosody, and as noted, Clough and other Victorian poets experimented with it as the basis of other poetic forms. Arnold had experimented with the hexameter when translating Homer: this is a 6-foot line used by Homer and Vergil, and Arnold's experiments with it were not successful as he himself owned, though it can be used for comic and satirical effect – as in Clough's 'The Bothie' or Longfellow's 'Evangeline'.

In both 'Thyrsis' and 'The Scholar-Gypsy' Arnold uses the pentameter, the 5-footer, as the basic metrical unit of a 10 line stanza. This stanza appears to be of Arnold's own creation, a sestet (6 lines) with the sixth line shortened to three stresses, followed by the first four lines of a Petrarchan sonnet. As in other ways it has affiliations with the 'Ode to a Nightingale'. The rhyme scheme closely follows the visual pattern of the line insets, each differing length of inset following each different changing rhyme scheme save where the length of inset would be too great i.e. in the last four lines (the quatrain), in which case the rhyme pattern but not its difference is visually repeated. The sixth line with the fewer stresses is the odd one out, acting as both brake and accelerator to the rhythmic paragraphs on either side, and as such, marks either the syntactic end to the sestet or the start of a new subject for the following quatrain.

abcbc a deed – rhyme scheme
abcbc d bccb – inset scheme

Here then is the invocation: to his own grief that it may evoke the memory of Clough, hidden both within himself and in the Cumnor Hills. Arnold has stretched the ancient convention to accommodate present psychology and Berkshire nature. The very first stanza signals this link between past and present in its reference to Sibylla – the eternal but ageing Sibyl, prophetess of Christ, and the pub landlady of Arnold's youth, Sybella Curr, landlady of The Cross Keys Inn in South Hinksey, unfortunately now closed down. She died in 1860, a year before Clough. The classical gods have gone with Arnold's youth, and the present merely chronicles the bitterness of change, mental, economic and natural. If the pathetic fallacy will not suffice then the old gods cannot be invoked, and Arnold alone must create eternity through his own poetic inspiration. Thus Arnold is Clough's only mourner, for the quest for truth is solitary, a matter of conscience and often seen as inimical by society:

> He wends unfollowed, he must house alone;
> Yet on he fares, by his own heart inspired.
> (209-210)

The land of the Golden Age

This comprises two lands in 'Thyrsis' – the land of their youth and the land of the 17th century scholar-gypsy. This latter is the land before industrialisation, as was Oxford in the 1840s, still medieval in outlook, ceremony and architecture. We notice the paucity of reference to modernity in both 'The Scholar-Gypsy' and 'Thyrsis' save for what the two poets escape from – the harsh din of the city.

In 'The Scholar-Gypsy' the land of the Golden Age, whose dual concept is summed up in the Vergilian notion of Arcadia, is entered

123

through stanza 3 where the narrator, drowsy in a shaded August bower, almost partakes of an opium dream of scarlet poppies and air-swept lindens and,

> … perfumed showers
> Of bloom on the bent grass where I am laid
> (27-8)

The hot summer day and the nearness of Glanvil's book about the scholar-gypsy hint at a near-death experience (notice the passive form of "where I am laid," as if in death) or at least of his falling asleep, with the story's last-remembered images as the stimuli acting on his poetic imagination. It is no coincidence that Lewis Carroll's Alice, 12 years later, undergoes the same rite of passage in this figurative method of describing one's entry into the otherworld, a method which had been in place since medieval times. Dunbar (fl. 1490) had satirised it in his "The Tretis of The Tua Mariit Wemen and the Wedo" where the narrator's entry into the hidden summer garden is foiled by hawthorns and he remains stuck voyeuristically while the gay ladies exchange vicious sexist gossip. This world once entered is not easy to leave save by a wrench: "But what – I dream!" (135). The scholar-gypsy does not feel the passing of time but the narrator does, and this lack of empathy between the two is highlighted by the immediate reference to modernity and its moral incertitudes.

'Thyrsis' similarly follows the temporal plot of 'The Scholar-Gypsy' in its evocative journey through time and space (English season, English landscape) into the Arcadian dreamworld. It is entered through Arnold's remembrance of his youth – now his visits are rare, now his memory of each field is dim, but then he knew each flower and knew every herder and ploughman. This world of youth, which each of us glosses with a time of happiness and home-safety before we are cast like corks onto the tide of self-preservation and the growing cynicism of age, of "unkept promises and broken hearts" as Betjeman says, is urged on by half-remembered conversations with Clough about Glanvil and the Gypsy Scholar. It is here (33) at the very start of the poem that the link is made between the scholar-gypsy and the signal-elm, and the land that both are rooted in is entered in the next stanza in Arcadian terms:

Here, too, our shepherd pipes we first assayed.

This land contains both the cycle of the seasons (which even at their wildest are no foe to man) and, ominously, the inheritance of Bion's death in Arnold's despair of this world.

Between "Thou hearest the immortal chants of old" (181) to "And all the marvel of the golden skies" (190) of stanza 19 Arnold describes in a series of formulaic – in their use as referential shortcuts – yet vivid images the golden land Clough retreats to ("There thou art gone" – line 191), the time before man's contamination of the world, but also a land that contains not only death in the shape of Lityerses but resurrection in Daphnis' springing from the fountain of life into the golden skies. Yeats' 'Ancestral Houses' (from *Meditations in Time of Civil War*) has a similar appeal to the golden land in its theme of the passing of an age of aristocratic aestheticism, many of the key words of stanza 19 of 'Thyrsis' being echoed in particular by the second stanza: "sprang/sprung, marvel/marvellous, fountain/ fountain" (and earlier "jet"), but Yeats recognises that bringing Arcadia into the mortal world corrupts its former greatness of achievement with the taint of human envy and bitterness. Arnold keeps the golden land out of human reach.

It is worth reiterating that the golden land which Vergil embodied in his Arcadia was not yet another version of heaven or utopia – it was the platonic ideal of nature given a name and a place that linked it tenuously to this world. Heaven is morality's eternal prize whereas utopia is evolution's mortal prize, dependant on one's political interpretation of it. Arcadia is youth and immortality, but its sensuality means that the accident of death is ever present. In this golden land the gods play at mortals as shepherds (much as Marie-Antoinette did on her toy farm), where nature regulates herself through the vibrancy of youth, the nymphs and lesser gods, those life-forces sprung from earth and water. Age and death disturbed this balance, thus the necessity for divine rebirth and the restoration of the ideal. As in the pastorally described Eden of *Paradise Lost*, this was a world halfway between god and man, where man not only had empathy with nature but a regard for its deeper spiritual meaning that in the classical world was to be expressed through the Eleusinian mysteries.

This was that nobler, safer, world that held such attraction for Arnold. But like Vergil's Arcadia this was a world with the drudgery taken out of it; here there is none of the sweat of nature so clearly expressed in Horace's bucolic poetry. Arnold thought lowly of country life, and he preferred the academic life of the cloister or the grace of the London salons to Fox Howe and the Lakes. At his retirement he did not retreat to the country – no rose-clad cottage called Dunroamin for him, he was too sardonic to believe the hoped-for idyll could ever come true. The country life was hard and at heart he was a city-man, with its ensuing contradictions: society he enjoyed, its cultural attitudes he did not. His personal Arcadia was strictly of the imagination, uncoloured by childhood dreams yet glossed with youth's memories. The death of his father when Matthew was nineteen and his mother's removal to wild Westmoreland quickly sobered his entry into adulthood. Thus Berkshire Doricness could be personalised, modernised, brought nearer to the Victorian version of Arcadia as depicted in Morris' *News from Nowhere*, the garden-city with both function and relevance.

Its opposite was the world only hinted at in 'Thyrsis', that one between man and devil with its Blakean grinding down of belief, imagination and old certitudes, its "harsh, heart-wearying roar" (234) – the modern world of Manchester. This industrial world and its offspring, the materialists and machinists, the evolutionists, the Nietzscheans, the social theorists, are totally rejected in 'Thyrsis'. Arnold makes no comparison between the two worlds save by implication, condemnatory in its unspokenness, as we shall see below.

The dead man as youthful friend and fellow poet (with friends disguised as shepherds)

The first verse follows the tradition of including characterisation of author and friend begun by Theocritus in his 'Idyll 7'. The Thyrsis of the title had previously appeared in 'Idyll I – The Passion of Daphnis' and Vergil's 'Eclogue VI'. He was also the Attendant Spirit (in shepherd's guise) in Milton's masque of the Ludlow woods, 'Comus':

Who with his soft pipe and smooth-dittied song,
Well knows to still the wild winds when they roar,
And hush the waving woods.

(86-8)

Here Thyrsis represents the rational, beneficent Apollonian side
of nature as opposed to the Dionysiac Comus of the title. In Arnold's
poem Thyrsis not only carries over this Apollonian (or Parnassian)
quality but takes us straight into the heart of the pastoral convention:
Here, too, "our shepherd-pipes we first assay'd ... My pipe is lost ...
But Thyrsis of his own will went away." Thyrsis 'went away' because
the Apollonian Clough – whom Arnold thought too idealistic and
intense in many of his beliefs and that he should have learnt to live
with the prosaic facts of life – could not intellectually subscribe to
the Thirty-nine Articles and had to give up his fellowship at Oriel.

Arnold and Clough, "we swains" of Spenserian pedigree, were
of course poetic rivals who occasionally sniped at one another's
poetry; Theocritus wrote idylls describing poetic contests between
shepherds and their like, such as 'Damoetas and Daphnis' and to a
lesser extent 'The Reapers', which reproduced the Lityerses Song.
Other references to the Arcadian life include Proserpina, Sicily, the
immortal chants of old, Corydon who first appears in Theocritus'
'Idyll IV', Daphnis, Lityerses, and "silly sheep". Corydon – a
shepherd in Vergil's 'Eclogue VIII' who beat Thyrsis in a poetic
contest – is the sniping Arnold in disguise; he was also aped by
Hobbinol the clownish in 'The Shepheardes Calendar', and may thus
reflect Arnold's subconscious suspicion of plagiarism. But Arnold,
though judgemental of Clough's poetry (accusing him of not cutting
a "smoother reed," perhaps a reference to the 'Romantic' incoherence
in Clough's poetry), is generous to his friend – "Time, not Corydon,
hath conquered thee."

The phrase "silly sheep" has its source in Spenser's 'Daphnaida'.
In Elizabethan English 'silly' still retained its earliest meaning of
harmless or blessed, though Arnold, simultaneously using it in its
ancient and modern senses for greater effect (a Miltonic stylistic
device perfected in *Paradise Lost*), uses its modern meaning of
frivolous to hint at the unreality of Arcadia. Already we suspect that
the traditional form of the pastoral elegy – though a fitting form – is
not the key to soothe Arnold's grief.

The motif of the lost or broken pipe can signify not just the passing of youth but grief and despair: in 'The Shepheardes Calendar' Colin cannot please Rosalinde so "broke his aten pipe, and down dyd lye". The classical piping in 'Thyrsis' also links Arnold and Clough to their Victorian present: the path they so often trod to the signal-elm runs past the mass of reeds that grows in the present day nature reserve of Happy Valley, between South Hincksey and Childsworth Farm. The conventional demands of dead-young-poet-as-shepherd mourned by friend-as-shepherd are thus fully met. But this is a shepherd who has forsaken Arcadia:

> He went; his piping took a troubled sound
>   Of storms that rage outside our happy ground;
> He could not wait their passing, he is dead.
>   (48-50)

And what of dialect? The narrator as Doric shepherd conventionally, though not always, assumed the Doric dialect, but as we have noted of 'Thyrsis', Arnold's modernisation of the pastoral has muted its conventions almost to the point of disappearance, and we must continually scrape away the top contexts to uncover its ancient foundations. Discounting poetic archaicisms conventional to the time such as 'thou' and 'hath,' and a few infelicities of grammar and rhythm that can hardly be claimed as Oxford Doric, his championing of the grand style forestalled the obvious use of dialect; but Arnold supplies enough hints to remind us of the tradition. We have seen in "silly sheep" his Miltonic use of semantics; it is seen again in "we swains" (Elizabethan shepherds but Victorian persons of no repute: "it was a peasant's life" he once remarked of the countryside), conscious irony no doubt in view of his and Clough's fame. More obvious because visual (like the line insets of each stanza), are the seemingly misspelt place-names: Ensham for Eynsham, Cumner for Cumnor, Chilswell for Childsworth. To these should be added Sibylla, a conscious misspelling of Sybella Curr to link us visually to the classical Sibyll.

If the linguistic evidence is slight the dialect of geography is stronger. It is impossible to divorce the land from its geology, the canal and railway cuttings that dissected it to reveal its stratigraphy. Crowned by Wytham and Hurst hills, here is a wooded loop of land almost surrounded by the Thames to the west of Oxford which it overlooks from its highpoints. The new railway with its long sidings and cuttings ran alongside the Thames, bringing with it the anti-Arcadia of subsidiary industries and housing, all sprung up between Arnold's leaving Oxford in 1847 and Clough's death in 1861. "How changed is here each spot man makes or fills!" – he says in the very first line, but overt reference to this clamourous new world as noted above is denied us. In 'The Scholar-Gypsy' of 1853 he equates somewhat paradoxically the spread of the industrial revolution and its Mancunian logic with the coming of a "merry Grecian coaster" (243), but save for this tenuous reference no concession is made to the modern landscape in either pastoral.

'Thyrsis' is firmly rooted in the Berkshire countryside of their youth (now part of Oxfordshire, due to changes in county boundaries in 1974), from Hinksey in the first stanza to Hurst in the twenty-second, from pubs and weirs to farmsteads and "haunts beloved". "I cannot describe the effect which this landscape always has upon me – the hillside with its valleys, and Oxford in the great Thames valley below," he wrote in 1885. It is a land rich in geological resonance. In 1840 the Ice Age arrived with the Hungry Forties when William Buckland, Professor of Geology at Oxford, tested Hutton's theory of glacial drift by examining evidence in the Lake District. That the earth could be vastly older than prevailing religious thought allowed, caused a huge controversy that was only settled in 1863. Ice ages vastly effect sea levels and thus the speed and courses of rivers. Proof of these changes was provided by the 'Thames Terraces,' "Above by Ensham, down by Sandford" (115). Between these two spots are Wolvercote and Summertown just to the north of Oxford, two of the three Thames Terraces or classic geological features formed by the deposition of sediment then by the speeding up and eating back of the river as sea-levels rose and fell through four Ice Ages.

James Hutton had established the principles of stratification and rock formation in his *Theory of Earth*, 1785, and these principles were reiterated in 1833 by Charles Lyell in his *Principles of Geology*. He asserted that geological change, due to processes that had happened in the seas, rivers and lakes, was ongoing and thus similar to ('uniform with') those of our own time. This theory of uniformitarianism also became the basis of Darwinian evolution theory and archaeological excavation. All these intellectual upheavals were uppermost in Arnold's mind – and visual in the new Oxford below him – when he visited Old Boar's Hill in 1862 and first conceived the plan of 'Thyrsis', but they function not merely to provide a dark contrast to the poem's colours but, as we shall see, to provide a solid if hidden foundation for its theme of the decay of a brighter and less mechanical age. As such, the railway-scoured countryside is ignored in favour of a Berkshire Doricness, the city noise for sheep-bells. And a Sicily transferred to an idyllic Berkshire makes the pastoral convention more credible to his audience – for as he says of Proserpine:

> ... of our poor Thames she never heard!
> Her foot the Cumner cowslips never stirr'd:
> And we should tease her with our plaint in vain!
> (97-100)

The dead man's persona is that of the dying god

The importance of the first stanza cannot be overstated: here is the plot of the journey through space, time and season, the theme of decay and age, the melancholic 'ubi sunt', the introduction of the dead poet as classical shepherd – and here is Sibylla who like the Cumaean sibyl will lead us into the underworld, imaginatively if not personally. "Thyrsis and I" takes us into the pastoral convention; Sibylla takes us into the elegiac convention (as she was also to do in *The Waste Land)*. The sibyl was both one and many; immortal without the gift of eternal youth yet doomed eventually to die. Their oracles or Sibylline leaves, that were kept in the Temple of Jupiter at Rome, were of less value to later ages than their supposed prophesying of the birth of Christ (Vergil, 'Bucolics IV'). The irony of masking her as Sybella Curr, pub landlady, suggests that change, not perpetuity, is the natural order, that the Classical gods are powerless in the face of decay, that the 'pathetic fallacy' will not suffice. Gone Sibylla's name and with it any faith in an unchangingly cyclical world. If Clough is Adonis he will not show himself so plainly as Bion's dying god, nor so starkly on his bier as Lycidas or Adonais.

In fact, the dying god is hidden everywhere – in floral reference, in reference to other elegies, even hidden in language play as for example in the lines:

> Humid the air! Leafless, yet soft as spring,
> The tender purple spray on copse and briers!
>
> (17-18)

where, in a winter that is spring, the tender purple spray on copse and briers suggests the phonetic similarity of 'corpse and bier,' that here is Clough as Adonis, dead on his flower-strewn litter. The purple spray then not only resonates as the unseen mourners' wish for his rebirth, but also carries this resonance forward to the "purple fritillaries" (107) and "spikes of purple orchises" (115), themselves adding to the subliminal imagery with their own language of folklore: the fritillary is the pride of May (and of the water-meadows of Magdalen College), the crown imperial that looks back to Proserpine's "crowned hair" of flowers (88) and forward to winter decay in "the coronals of that forgotten time" (117). The orchid with its testicle shape is a plant of sexual implication (*vide* orchidectomy), and was used in love potions. Its leaves give the appearance of having been stained by blood, and so this coded language of flowers tells us that the goddess of spring has lost her royal lover to winter. More obvious as a reference to Adonis is line 55: "With blossoms red and white of fallen May." Not only is fallen May a metaphor for Adonis but the red and white blossoms are the anemone that fades in May, and the anemone was the sacred flower of Adonis, his blood and dead flesh. This line looks forward to anemones in flower till May (199) where they now take on the added allusion of Clough reborn as the Scholar-Gypsy. Again we see the corpse on the bier but risen into becoming an integral part of the poem's meaning.

Allusions to other elegies, notably the 'Lament for Bion' and 'Adonais', are readily seen. For instance, the finality of death: "Yes, thou art gone!" (140) echoes lines 104-5 of the 'Lament for Bion'; "Thyrsis never more we swains shall see" (83) reminds us of "He will awake no more, oh, never more!" ('Adonais', VIII, 1) or 'Lycidas' "Now thou art gone, and never must return!" with their blunt dismissal of the pathetic fallacy. Again, Shelley's structuring of cyclical inevitability by depicting spring as autumn:

> Grief made the young Spring wild, and she threw down
> Her kindling buds, as if she Autumn were;
>
> ('Adonais', XVI, 1-2)

suggests the plot of seasonal movement in 'Thyrsis': "This winter-eve is warm ... soft as spring" (16), where Arnold wishes to move forward in time to summer blooms and fecundity to make-believe a Clough reborn as nature's youth. Shelley moves closer to the convention of pastoral elegy by hinting that autumn and the death of Adonis are now upon us. The implication in each poem is that the cycle brings both death and life, eternally and repetitively, as we have seen in Yeats' 'Her Vision in the Wood'. The problem in both is that the reappearance of life, if successful, may not take a form we can recognise let alone communicate with.

More of the floral symbolism (Arnold had a deep knowledge of flowers as we shall see) and elegiac reference is discussed below, and no doubt the reader will find his own links, so I shall restrict my exploration of the Dying God persona to the two stanzas (lines 81-90 and 181-190) that overtly make us aware of Clough as Adonis:

> Alack, for Corydon no rival now! –
> But when Sicilian shepherds lost a mate,
> Some good survivor with his flute would go,
> Piping a ditty sad for Bion's fate;
> And cross the unpermitted ferry's flow,
>   And relax Pluto's brow,
> And make leap up with joy the beauteous head
> Of Proserpine, among whose crowned hair
> Are flowers first open'd on Sicilian air,
> And flute his friend, like Orpheus, from the dead.
>   (81-90)

Proserpine as symbol of seasonal rebirth had long been invoked as the bringer of fertility, but why not her male version here, Attis or Adonis? Arnold is appealing to classical precedent by summoning up the poetic image of Sicily, birthplace of Theocritus and Ceres' favourite spot because of its fertility. It was also the setting for Bion's and Moschus's pastorals. Bion was the subject of Moschus' 'Lament for Bion', lines 115-126 of which are closely paralled in the extract above. The approach to Clough as Adonis is thus by indirect pedigree – through Bion, first poet to be portrayed as the dying god, and through Proserpina, herself reborn each spring. Sicily cements these references in the form of the classical pastoral that Arnold is working in.

Of course Proserpine never trod amongst the Cumner cowslips, and Clough is become no Mediterranean deity but a representative of it, much like the spirit of classicism becomes its greatest expression – a vase – in Keats' 'Ode on a Grecian Urn'. As in Adonais we are taken beyond the reassuring if fallible notion of the dying god into the life-force beyond. And as the 'Lament for Bion' tells us, the flowers may die and grow again another year, but humanity sleeps long and unawaking, as Arnold is forced to recognise in Clough's "morningless and unawakening sleep" (169):

> Thou hearest the immortal chants of old! –
>   Putting his sickle to the perilous grain
>   In the hot cornfield of the Phrygian king,
>   For thee the Lityerses-song again
>   Young Daphnis with his silver voice doth sing;
>   Sings his Sicilian fold,
>   His sheep, his hapless love, his blinded eyes –
>   And how a call celestial round him rang,
>   And heavenward from the fountain-brink he sprang,
>   And all the marvel of the golden skies.
>
> (181-200)

The Lityerses myth has been discussed above. Arnold felt sensitive enough about its possible incomprehension to his readers that a note explaining its allusions was added to the 1869 edition. From the elegy of Adonis re-born in the spring crop we move into the darker landscape of human sacrifice amongst "the perilous grain". The yellow hot cornfield becomes the warm golden skies – the corn's soul may be renewable in this world but man's soul is renewable only in our concept of the next and all its "marvel of the golden skies". For Daphnis, the divine sacrifice of and for Lityerses, sings his own death-song, but is taken heavenward in death and not as he doubtless expected earthward as corn-spirit, for his song is a Theocritan pastoral. We should note the lack of verb in line 201 that gives it such impact, a Blakean stylistic device as in the "What dread hand? & what dread feet?" of 'The Tyger': this performs the same function as the coda at the end of 'Sohrab and Rustum', where the reader is forced to create his own poetic world both independent of, yet still tenuously linked to, the foregoing passages that have helped create it.

By analogy – and the analogy is not straightforward because Arnold has merged three different versions of the Daphnis myth, another reason for his note to the 1869 edition – Clough, for whom Daphnis is imagined singing this song, is both Daphnis the divine sacrifice and Daphnis the heaven-rewarded poet. By implication the dying god has escaped the eternal seasonal cycle of his own death and rebirth, and in the next stanza (191-200) we move into that imagined world of the scholar-gypsy and towards the resolution of the poem.

The procession of the mourners

As in the 'Epic of Gilgamesh' the mourners in 'Thyrsis' are both non-existent and ever-present, and noticeably in this respect the poem makes a change both purposeful and important in the traditional structure as followed by its well-known forerunners. So it is worthwhile to explore how this next characteristic of the pastoral elegy – the procession of mourners – works in two of the classic English pastoral elegies.

'Thyrsis' is usually compared with 'Lycidas' and 'Adonais', these two poems being regarded as the most representative forms of the pastoral elegy. Other pastoral elegies fall short of the recognised convention in important aspects. 'Astrophel', for example, makes no use of the personae of grieving friends, the narrator's emotions are nowhere made explicit, Astrophel suffers the same death as Adonis but the link between the two is not made till the very end, and then only tenuously. Whitman's 'When Lilacs Last in the Dooryard Bloomed', an elegy on Abraham Lincoln written at the same time as 'Thyrsis', even with its floral and seasonal imagery makes few concessions to the pastoral elegy form. *The Waste Land* is overtly an ironic commentary on the convention's form and underlying beliefs. Such differences, of course, warn us how varied the form of the pastoral elegy can be. And as we have seen, Arnold in 'Thyrsis' is his own mourner, his own tormentor, yet invoking the past of the natural landscape to lament with him as he undergoes his processional journey into night.

In 'Lycidas' the procession begins with the appearance, one after the other, of individual Classical, pseudo-Classical and Christian figures – the fountain nymph Arethusa, Neptune's herald, the sage

Hippotades, Camus the pseudo-god of the River Cam, i.e. the University of Cambridge, and St Peter. The procession as such comprises Alpheus the river-god of Arcadia, and the Sicilian Muse (Persephone or perhaps Alpheus' lost love Arethusa) who is invoked to bring the gods of the vales and bid them enact the mourners' ritual function:

> To strew the laureate hearse where Lycid lies.
> For so, to interpose a little ease,
> Let our frail thoughts dally with false surmise.
> (151-153)

The "false surmise", or pathetic fallacy as Ruskin termed it, came about when at the end of his '5th Eclogue', a tearful lament for nature, Vergil introduced songs of joy. Christian writers took over this theme, Classical figures were adapted to Christian concepts, and the pastoral elegy was aimed towards proving that man did not live in a hostile universe. We can see Milton representing his friend Edward King (Lycidas), who was drowned crossing the Irish Sea, as Adonis who was ritually placed on a raft, drowned and then reborn. The pathetic fallacy is reconciled with reality when Classical belief is reinterpreted as Christian creed:

> Weep no more, woeful shepherds, weep no more,
> For Lycidas, your sorrow, is not dead,
> Sunk though he be beneath the wat'ry floor ...
> So Lycidas sunk low, but mounted high,
> Through the dear might of Him that walked the waves.
> (165-173)

But the pathetic fallacy of the mourners – their need to hold onto their dead in hope of its earthly rebirth – is still catered for:

> Now, Lycidas, the shepherds weep no more;
> Henceforth thou art the Genius of the shore.
> (182-3)

King is doubly resurrected, both as Christian soul in heaven and as minor deity on earth. Thus the mourners represent pure human grief and its inability to accept the cold reality of death. As such they are the representatives of the women mourners who partook in the ritual of the Dying God, slashing their breasts and tearing their hair. This function in Milton and Shelley is superseded by the private mourners who both partake in and comment on the emotions of death, and hint towards a meaningful resolution.

Shelley claimed to be an atheist and so the dead Keats in 'Adonais' becomes the universal spirit behind nature, while the mourners' pathetic fallacy is realised by allowing the grosser aspects of nature to renew themselves in yearly cycles. But the reality is that the dead do not return to us; reborn though they may be, it is into a different world:

> ... oh, dream not that the amorous Deep
> Will yet restore him to the vital air;
> Death feeds on his mute voice, and laughs at our despair.
>
> (III, 7-9)

The procession of mourners is more concrete, more fully described and thematically linked to the poem, yet less obviously Classical or Christian than that in Milton. The mourners represent almost every aspect of life: the muse Urania, Keats' spiritual mother, "Most musical of mourners", the dreams of Keats rising from his corpse as poetic spirits denying the fact of death – "Our love,our hope, our spirit is not dead", various emotions and thoughts of Keats like sorrow, fantasies and sighs, the wild winds, Pleasure, the morning that:

> Came in slow pomp ...
> Like pageantry of mist on an autumnal stream.
>
> (XIII, 8-9)

Another mourner is spring, intimately linked to the theme of seasonal death:

> Grief made the young Spring wild and she threw down
> Her kindling buds,as if she Autumn were ...
> For whom should she have waked the sullen year?
>
> (XVI, 1-4)

and Echo, eagle, Albion, nightingale, the mountain shepherds, and finally Shelley himself appears. The pathetic fallacy is satisfied:

He lives, he wakes – 'tis Death is dead, not he:
Mourn not for Adonais.

                          (XLI, 1-2)

but the drawback is that though Keats lives again he does so not in
our sight but in the unseen power that surges through nature:

Spreading itself where'er that Power may move
Which has withdrawn his being to its own.

                          (XLII, 6-7)

The spirits of other poets young in death – Chatterton, Sydney,
Lucan – arise from oblivion and acclaim him king of the heaven of
song. For heaven to Shelley is not a dream but pure thought and
energy, this life a tyranny of grossness and nightmare. "He hath
awakened from the dream of life" (XXXIX, 2). This is a reversal of
the ancient world's concept of life – that existence in this world was
preferable to that in the next where we would exist merely as thirsty
wandering shades. In Shelley's almost Blakean vision established
Christianity has no place in either world and ironically the pathetic
fallacy does exist, but only in the 'real' world of death, a reality we
are encouraged to seek: – Die,

If thou wouldst be that which thou dost seek!
Follow where all is fled! ...

                          (LII, 6-7)

The soul of Adonais, like a star,
Beacons from the abode where the Eternal are.

                          (LV, 8-9)

In terms of poetic form Shelley acknowledges a twofold debt, to
Milton in the poem ("the Sire of an immortal strain,/ Blind, old, and
lonely") and to Moschus in the preface ("Moschus, epitaph. Bion").
Thematically the Platonic ideal is hinted at in the preface as a source
of the poem's resolution, though the quotation from Plato (of the
dead man in life shining like the morning star, in death shining like
the evening star) is little more than a conventional description of the
dead to console the living. But the meaning of 'dead' has a marked
difference in both poems – Lycidas has risen in Christ but Adonais

becomes the spirit of nature, going beyond the hill-walking spirit of Bion to invigorate not just the gross earth but the ethereal universe.

These differences arise from the separate functions of the mourners. In 'Lycidas' they provide not just the ritualistically beautiful but also the internal tension necessary for the poem's resolution; in 'Adonais' they function both as Shelley's conscience and as all-embracing symbols of nature and its life force. In both poems they perform the structural – and descriptive – role of heralding the rebirth of spring with flower-strewing, but in Adonais the flower-strewing – the sympathetic magic of rebirth – becomes the bestowing of true life on the corpse, for each of the mourners are "mirrors of/ The fire for which all thirst," strewing the universal light of eternity, each like Adonais:

> ... a portion of the loveliness
> Which once he made more lovely.
> (XLIII, 1-2)

Milton's mourners are strictly relevant to the event, their individuality subservient to their metaphoric function, St Peter (who witnessed Christ's walking on the water) accompanied by Classical river gods and naiads, more in line with the rites of Adonis and the facts of King's death by drowning. Milton allows St Peter to speak the diatribe of bitterness; in 'Adonais' Shelley's own persona – that of the embittered poet in mourning – performs this function. Milton is not part of the procession, though his persona is that of an observant shepherd; Shelley is both part of the procession (but not as a shepherd) and detached narrator. For Milton, the mourners i.e. the Classical gods have failed to answer death ("Return, Alpheus, the dread voice is past/ That shrunk thy streams") but their meaning is taken over by Christianity – resurrection comes through Christ, and Classical allusions become part of Christian salvation.

Milton uses two structural elements to distinguish the Classical mourners from the Christian – the Vergilian eclogue to highlight the pagan fallacy, and the Italian canzone as used by Sannazaro and in 'The Shepheardes Calender' to express the Christian aspects. King (Lycidas) combines the two elements as a saint above and imagined tutelary spirit below, enabling Milton to go forward with renewed hope:

> Tomorrow to fresh woods and pastures new.
> (193)

Milton – cleansed of grief – returns strengthened to his life; Shelley sees no beauty in a brutal world and looks forward to the purity of his own death. Arnold realises the search for a meaning to existence is to be found not in man's crude and momentary monuments to his own delusions but in its natural expression.

For in 'Thyrsis' Arnold may be the chief mourner – the only human mourner – but his processional companions are the natural outgrowth of this world, the flowers and woods, the water and night, that stand not only as elegiac metaphors but also as literalisms of their own individual yet cyclical existence. They are the proof of natural rebirth and as such inhabit a dimension beyond our human experience of one world only. They are both signifier and signified; they mourn Clough because he is human and cannot be reborn as they can; they grieve for humanity and its solitary existence which they have been liberated from. They are the waving, unweeping, mourners of all of us, ever around us, ever silent. As if to nature we ourselves are the dead.

Flower and water imagery

Flowers

We enter now into the realm of symbolism, another land whose language is unlocked not by reference to dictionaries – "genuine poetry is conceived and composed in the soul" (*Essays in Criticism*) – but by an intuition somehow experienced, a déjà vu of a parallel world, that other realities can be revealed from a merging of signifier and signified. A world, as Yeats said in 'Among School Children', where we cannot know the dancer from the dance.

As noted above, some words have an innate symbolism that bypasses contextual translation and strikes directly at the core of our imagination. Certain flowers, water and trees in general, mist and night – all have a connotation that derives from what is felt to be a natural similarity to mood or emotion. One could almost say that such innate symbolism gave rise to myth. In effect such words in natural speech act as both denoters and metaphors, and often without our realising it. Expressions such as 'over the hill and far away' and

'I wish it was night and I was home in bed' have a power far beyond their literal meaning: they are gateways into an archetypal world. Flowers have been symbols of grief and rebirth, and water of the source of life, its beginning and end, since the dawn of civilisation. Such metaphoric words are the very stuff of poetry and every poet knows it. Flowers and water, of course, are integral to the imagery of the pastoral elegy. But Arnold does not just throw a catalogue of flowers at us (as I suspect Shelley did) as if to say: 'these stand for death and rebirth as we all know – the rest is just poetic desciptiveness.' He went deeper and chose his flowers specifically for the occasion.

But was Arnold learned in the symbolism and etymology of the plants he was naming? By extension, did he know the history and psychology behind the myths of Greece that he used, or their link to Oxford and Berkshire? Many of his poems, like 'The Scholar-Gypsy' or 'A Dream' (1853), show his deep love for flowers and natural imagery, and his close observation of them, their species and environment: concerning 'Thyrsis' Arnold wrote to his mother that "the images are from actual observation … The cuckoo on the wet June morning I heard in the garden at Woodford, and all these three stanzas you like [lines 57-86 with their lush floral descriptions] are reminiscences of Woodford." We have seen in 'Lines Written in Kensington Gardens' how his use of arboreal symbolism refines and concretises nature. Lines 105-110 of 'Thyrsis' with their stress on Arnold's knowledge of the local flora is backed up by his statement that, on one walk near Wantage in 1861, just after Clough's death, "I got down into the meadows below Iffley, and filled my hands with fritillaries, half of them white ones." The truth is that wild flowers and their study were a lifelong passion with him, and he regularly corresponded with a Mr Gibson in Saffron Walden, Essex, on questions of identification.

His lists of flowers are strictly relevant to the season he is describing; in the two stanzas comprising lines 111-130, for instance, we see not only seasonal relevance but the floral symbolism of death further reinforced by the innate sybolism we have noticed above, the plough, the ferryman (boatman's daughter) and the grim reaper (the mowers – Lityerses with scythe suspended above the river). These two stanzas are superbly economic in Arnold's use of differing symbols to reinforce and add to one another's poetic power. The flowery dingle once so familiar has now been ploughed up (by Alexandrian convention the ploughboy was opposed to the pastoral shepherd and stood for the reality of hard work), the cowslips and orchises ploughed under, only the primroses left – "orphans of the flowery prime". These are flowers that like Adonis have bloomed and faded in May, the season Arnold is imagining at this point in the poem; like the corn-spirit they have been returned to earth for rebirth next year, only the primrose has been spared, the flower sacred to the muse as Donne well knew when he celebrated it in 'The Primrose'. Folklore asserts that a cowslip planted upside-down (or ploughed under) turns into a primrose. Coincidence or not, we have here a marvellous metaphor of natural death and rebirth within one reference.

The following stanza (121-130), by way of red loosestrife and blond meadowsweet (whose heavy scent could induce sleep unto death) – hardly of immediate impact to the unbotanically minded – is an 'ubi sunt' of the ferryman's daughter, the watching mowers, the journey down river of the youthful Clough and Arnold. Again, the flowers fit the season and the season fits the metaphors of death. "They all are gone, and thou art gone as well!" (130) – everything has become no more than this, an 'ubi sunt' of signifier and signified, and gone is the hope of resurrection, gone is the poet Clough, gone is Arnold's poetic activity, gone is the old world. Proserpine's "crowned hair" has become the "coronals of that forgotten time" (117) that cannot be resurrected in this modern world.

Similar cross-pollenating of flower season and symbol can be found in lines 23-29 of 'The Scholar-Gypsy', where August and its flowers (the poppies and perfumed showers of linden blossom) are used as a soporific gateway that leads us into the dreamworld of 17th century Oxford.

Arnold's assertion that he knows the flora, the landscape and the local people – 'I know' or its variants occurs six times in the poem – implies that he was conversant at least with the daily and seasonal customs of country life (in 'The Scholar-Gypsy' (82-3) he had noted how country girls in May come from the surrounding hamlets to dance around the Fyfield elm). Arnold is immersing himself in the landscape, asserting his link to nature and its cyclical rituals. "I cannot describe the effect which this landscape always has upon me." And beyond this country-knowledge is his acute awareness of the intellectual arguments of the time concerning man's non-religious origins, their desperate search to find a something better than ape and earthlier than angel.

Ruskin analysed various Shakespearean names such as Desdemona and Ophelia to try and elucidate the themes of Shakespearian tragedy. Arnold was scathing of such oblique analysis: "to give it that degree of prominence is to throw the reins to one's whim," he remarked. Yet on the other hand he could opine: "I will not say that the meaning of Shakespeare's names ... has no effect at all," realising – as we have seen from his use of "Sibylla" or "fritillary" or "copse and briers" – that hidden semantics can enrich poetic reality, a sentiment echoed in his preface to the second edition of his poems of 1854. Here he states that although the modern mind no longer has any direct affinity with Macbeth or Oedipus because of the historical and cultural gulf that separates us from the past (an evolutionary point of view in itself), those characters "can be made present by an act of poetic imagination" – heroic figures to express universal passions. For this was an age that was headily exploring the history and development of man's mind by way of the emerging science of social anthropology, centred around Darwin, Huxley (a friend and occasional critic of Arnold), E.B. Tylor and James (later Sir James) Frazer. Arnold witnessed at first hand the seasonal country rituals still very much alive before Frazer came to encode them in *The Golden Bough* (1890).

Frazer's view of mankind's psychological development was, naturally, evolutionary (it is worth noting that the pastoral elegy by its very nature is also evolutionary, both in its ability to adapt to temporal or spatial change and in its thematic movement). He described man as progressing from a belief in magic as a means of controlling his environment to religious belief as the means of placating the gods of nature. The next logical stage of development appeared to be scientific thought, and using scientific thought later psychologists like Freud used Frazer's ideas to explain the mentality of taboo and repression; Jung used him as authority for the facts behind his theory of the archetypes. This exploration of myth and folklore as expression of – and therefore the key to – psychic patterns reached its apogee in the early 20th century with the erudite works on classical literature of such scholars as Francis Cornford, Margaret Murray, Jane Harrison and Jessie Weston, the latter's theory on the cultural anthropology behind the Holy Grail legends suggesting to T.S. Eliot the symbolism that underpins *The Waste Land*.

So we can hardly say Arnold's use of symbolic language is fortuitous in that somehow he summoned up images whose full potential he did not know, much as to say that Shakespeare, with no degree in psychology, accidentally hit upon the mainsprings of human emotion. We have already noted that a catalogue of symbols can fulfil its function of signifying another reality, and that in the case of flowers Arnold's deep knowledge of their properties added to – and enlivened – their symbolic operation in a marvellously economic way. A symbol falls heavily if it is not handled well. To say, for instance, that the elm is both the symbol of truth and the goal of Arnold's journey is dismissive in its bareness – its symbolic value only shows its deep richness when handled in full knowledge of the possibilities inherent in all its realities of meaning within a particular context. Our delight in the symbolic language of 'Thyrsis' is deepened by our knowledge that Arnold was a classical scholar who was also historically and botanically literate; it is not lessened by our suspicion that maybe his interest in them was, Shelley-like, merely aesthetic for literary effect. Arnold well hid the conventional symbols he had to work with in their natural setting, but they bloom like fire when revealed.

Water

"One looks upon water as the Mediator between the inanimate and man," wrote Arnold to Clough from Switzerland. By this Arnold meant that water is the inanimate in motion, and the capital M of Mediator suggests the divinity of water, a very Celtic notion, that nebulous boundary between this world and the next. Classically, it represented the journey from this life to the underworld; in Christian terms, water symbolises baptism into a new awareness. Both these meanings are used in 'Thyrsis' as obvious references to death, but the main function of his watery symbolism is to keep us in mind of its Dying God associations as the rejuvenating agent of life, the dead Enkidu unlocking the waters of Uruk if you like. The water images of 'Thyrsis' link Adonis's death to his rebirth – the spring rain washing the red earth of Adonis' bloody flesh down the Cydnus to Biblos, his effigy thrown into the sea, his drowning and resurrection. This is most apparent in the Lityerses stanza, "And heavenward from the fountain brink he sprang" (200) where as remarked earlier, the leap is made from rebirth in nature to rebirth in heaven, the fountain (or spring of life) acting as a baptismal agent to enable Clough to escape the seasonal cycle and lead him from earthly darkness to spiritual bliss.

There are numerous watery references, either to the Thames that dominates the hilly landscape by its great encirclement of it, or to water in general. Linked to the Thames references (including Wytham flats) are two indirect allusions to Charon the Stygian ferryman. The "unpermitted ferry" (85) takes us forward to "the girl ... by the boatman's door" (121) who unmoors the skiff and pushes them into their underworld journey, past the mowers with raised scythes who all are gone (130), paralleling the journey-plots of winter to summer and youth to middle age. The mowers are an icon of death and finally mow themselves. It is no coincidence that the ferryman (or journey-into-hell) references occur between our glimpse of Adonis – dead on his bier with his primroses, "orphans of the flowery prime" (120) – and the Hades of the narrator's bitterness, where night:

> In ever-nearing circle weaves her shade.
> I see her veil draw soft across the day,
> I feel her slowly chilling breath invade
> The cheek grown thin, the brown hair sprent with grey;
> (132-35)

and one by one the senses close down till the hunters' hounds, the Cerberuses of the north, jar them awake and drive Arnold to the sanctuary ("I take the omen!" (161)) of the tree.

The tree

Think of a tree, its essentials, any tree. Its roots strike deep into the earth, its hiding boughs touch heaven. Think of famous trees – the one where the snake lived that stopped man from becoming God; the one Christ was crucified on to release man from evolution and launch him into godhead; the ash tree Woden hung himself from to gain universal understanding and self knowledge (thereby becoming the god of hangmen); or even the oak King Charles hid himself in to escape God's ideologists – some of these associations are immediate when we visualise a tree, some not. The more we are aware of them the richer our appreciation of their context – but the more aware we are the more we question the poet's knowledge of them, our possible anachronistic reading of them, his ability to control them. I trust I have already shown that Arnold knew his poetic business and realised that some symbols are universal across time and space in their psychological significance. I don't wish to belabour further his use of particular symbols, so I shall restrict discussion of the tree to lines 151-161.

Throughout the poem Arnold is climbing "to where the elm-tree crowns/The hill ... The signal-elm" (12/13,14). The tree is the binding symbol of 'Thyrsis', the search for it providing the plot of the poet's journey into past and future. For Arnold and Clough it symbolised the truth behind humanity's search for a secure faith (Clough considered he "could not honestly pursue Truth" by subscribing to the Thirty-nine Articles), the same symbolic effect operating in lines 29, 171, 176 and 254-256, showing that the search for truth, though arduous, is not hopeless:

> But hush! The upland hath a sudden loss
> Of quiet! – Look, adown the dusk hill-side,
>   A troop of Oxford hunters going home,
> As in old days, jovial and talking, ride!
>   From hunting with the Berkshire hounds they come.
>   Quick! Let me fly, and cross
> Into yon farther field! – 'Tis done; and see,
>   Back'd by the sunset, which doth glorify
>   The orange and pale violet evening sky,
> Bare on its lonely ridge, the Tree! The Tree!
>
> (151-160)

This is one of the great climaxes of the poem, packed with dark allusions that lead us finally to the tree. Besides Actaeon and Linus, hunted and torn apart by their own hounds, there is a reference to the Wild Hunt either of the night-sky (hobgoblins driving souls northward to hell) led by King Arthur, or of the Wild Hunt of the forest as it hunted lost souls "adown the dusk hill-side," usually led by Woden or Herne the hunter, a British oak-god, derived from the Celtic Cernunnos and used by Shakespeare in *The Merry Wives of Windsor*. The Wild Hunt was made famous by Walter Map in the story of Wild Edric of Shropshire, and by the Peterborough chronicler (*Anglo-Saxon Chronicle*, MS E) for the year 1127:

> ... *son þæræfter þa sægon and herdon fela men feole huntes hunten. Ða huntes wæron swarte and micele and ladlice, and here hundes ealle swarte and bradegede and ladlice, and hi ridone on swarte hors and on swart bucces... on ealle þa wudes... to Stanforde; and þa muneces herdon ða horn blawen þet hi blewen on nihtes. Soðfeste men heom kepten on nihtes...*
> (f.86)

Its positive aspect was the solitary wild hunter, the Wild Man, often portayed as outlawed or anti-social, with a sense of brooding power. Typically the Wild Man was someone who had retreated from this world into the forest of chaos, quest and self-knowledge – Merlin, Robin Hood, the Green Knight of medieval romance (who tested Arthur's court), Spenser's naturally noble Wild Man in 'The Faerie Queene'. To Frazer the Wild Man represents the resurrected Tree-spirit, and the Scholar-Gypsy is a type of Wild Man who out of isolation can teach us to re-orientate ourselves naturally, for our tree yet crowns the hill, and the tree on the ridge is his physical and spiritual refuge from the hunters. The Wild Man thus becomes a comment on civilisation, whether it be Enkidu by the waterholes of Sumer or a New Age traveller stoned in his caravan.

The tree is the end truth, and demolishes the foregoing pathetic fallacy of Clough reborn as Adonis. Here in the stanza's last line (160) is its climax, for beyond the death-hounds and the flight through the winter landscape and the dying god, highlighted by the sunset – itself a symbol of death and the dying day – stands on its hill the bare truth. "Quick! Let me fly" – as Granville's scholar was bid to do in 'The Scholar-Gypsy' – "our feverish contact fly!" (227) and fly our speech and smiles! (237). Arnold has become the Scholar-Gypsy of old, the explorer of the natural world he has created – the lone searcher, now that Clough is dead, for the truth, just as Clough later (237-240) assumes the scholar's spiritual mantle. This truth is an outgrowth of the poem's imagery which gives it substance and meaning – and concrete rationality to express the poem's theme – and this meaning I shall look at in a later section.

Such great trees as signal-elms, besides having supposedly magical power derived from their seasonal attributes, acted as gathering points, beacons or boundary markers; they were also used for hangings – 'Hangman's Bottom' in Bagley Wood, through which the Empress Maud fled, is a mile south of South Hinksey – and in early times were associated with Woden for reasons I have mentioned above. In terms of the poem's theme the elm-tree binds the spirit of Clough to the earth of Berkshire, a necessary interdependency in the quest for truth:

> Our friend, the Scholar-gypsy, was not dead;
> While the tree lived, he in these fields lived on.
> (29-30)

The Scholar-Gypsy – whose role is taken over physically by Arnold in 'Thyrsis' and then spiritually by the dead Clough – is here the embodiment of the tree-spirit, but whose life depended on that of the tree: if Arnold reaches the signal-elm the memory of Clough will dissolve and death will have won, cold and immutable and hopeless. Like truth it has to stand as a beacon on a hill difficult of access, physically enlightening but symbolically unreachable in its elusiveness of meaning. For the tree is the link between whatever earthly existence means and God's revelation of it, a meaning forever shifting in its dependency upon context: "the light we sought is shining still" (238).

As a rest from symbolism – its has the problem of gathering and compressing images into a ravelled core of interdependent meanings the nearer one gets to the resolution of a poem – and a diversion for those readers who wish to trace Arnold's journey past Chilswell farm, "the single elm-tree" was a conspicuous tree on Old Boar's Hill (not to be confused with the Fyfield elm). Near the so-called 'Matthew Arnold's Field' on Old Boar's Hill the thirsty walker (there is no pub nearer than the General Elliott in South Hinksey) will find Jarn Mound, an artificial hillock raised by Sir Arthur Evans the archaeologist, who lived nearby at Youlbury, to preserve "the view from Matthew Arnold's 'signal-elm' which looked towards the Isley Downs ... and ... Oxford." Evans raised a 50 feet high mound some 600 yards to the south-west of where the elm had stood, and being an archaeologist he placed a bowl of freshly minted coins in its foundations. A nature garden was created around the mound (he had also created a garden at his 'Villa Ariadne' base at Knossos). Like that hit by a volcanic eruption at 'House Delta' in Minoan Akrotiri the stairway up the mound has tilted and buckled, and I couldn't help but see here a wry symbolism of the poem's theme – change and decay and the collapse of old certainties. Uniformitarianism has caught up with Arnold's despair of it.

The narrator's self-pity and bitterness

The sharp, sensual imagery now gives way to typical Arnoldian austerity, world-weariness after the bright hopeful stanzas of youth, to despair then resigned observation of the nature of this world. As in 'Lycidas', Arnold pauses in the poem to look askance at contemporary events and attitudes. Both poets feel intimations of their own mortality – "And bid fair peace be to my sable shroud" ('Lycidas', 22), "And night as welcome as a friend would fall" ('Thyrsis', 150) – though each poet gives these sermonising episodes a different structural function. And whereas pastoral elegy uses its ritualisation to frame and absorb such critical thrusts, Eliot reverses this in *The Waste Land* to reveal an empty core of pastoral-turned-slagheap and dead ritual (for instance, Mr Eugenides the perverted Syrian Attis, the bed-sit typist as Aphrodite, the mourners drunk in an East End pub). Eliot's poem is an elegy for civilisation where the satire is turned inside out and the bowman becomes the victim of his own arrows; Arnold's is objective and thus can purge itself finally of its bitterness.

Such criticism or sermonising (and in 'Lycidas' the sermon has the added function of resolving the tension between pathetic fallacy and Christian resurrection, classicism and Augustinianism), which can range from diatribe to quiet musing, is used to propel the action forward from grief to reconciliation with the fact of death. Arnold's criticism consists of two groups each of two stanzas separated by the afterlife and resurrection of Clough. Stanzas 14 and 15 depict Arnold's grief and despair, stanzas 20 and 21 the reconciliation with the fact of Clough's death. And in stanza 22 whereas formerly Arnold had worn the mantle of the Scholar-Gypsy Clough now merges with that imagined figure and we move forward into the resolution.

Stanzas 14 and 15 – despair

Here the journey into the underworld passes through Arnold's despair (lines 131-150) then into the dual world of present-day Berkshire and classical Elysium – represented by the valley of the Arno where Clough died – till despair is transfigured by the tree and its spirit the Scholar-Gypsy, the "outliving thee" and the "anenomes in flower till May" that place Clough firmly on his death-litter with no hope of return, into the melancholic realisation that the quest for truth is solitary, everyman's journey alone through hell into light (191-210).

As Clough and Arnold sail into the underworld the narrator's bitterness emerges to carry the action forward on the intellectual plane. Deliberately, night frames these two stanzas (131-150) from "round me too the night" to "night as welcome as a friend". What is this bitterness? – the heaviness of approaching age and the fading of youth's hope, that insidiously suggest to Arnold the Keatsian ease of slipping into death. The nearing night and its chill (131) suggest the approach of age and this in turn leads Arnold's thoughts to the decline of youthful expectations. This is a favourite melancholic theme and the lines (146-7):

> Unbreachable the fort
> Of the long-batter'd world uplifts its wall

have analogues in a number of his poems, especially those also from the 1867 edition such as 'Palladium', 'Growing Old' and 'The Last Word' ("When the forts of folly fall,/ Find thy body by the wall!") where war and intellectual quest are seen in one another's terms, an Arnoldian association we have already seen in 'Dover Beach' ("where ignorant armies clash by night"). But typical Arnoldian restraint is applied to stop any degeneration of melancholy into a sentimentality and self-pity that would stop the poem in its tracks. The theme of retreat from human turmoil is also seen in another 1867 poem 'A Wish':

To feel the universe my home;
To have before my mind – instead

Of the sick room, the mortal strife,
The turmoil for a little breath –
The pure eternal course of life,
Not human combatings with death!
(43-48)

A statement of sentiment that reappears in the last two stanzas of 'Thyrsis' and its resolution.

The despair list seems conventional:

This does not come with houses or with gold,
With place, with honour, and a flattering crew;
(203-204)

but that is in accordance with the demands of the form. The list is simple, unembellished – in contrast to the rich profusion of imagery that frames the episode – and importantly this austere simplicity lifts the criticisms into universal generalisations that immediately sum up our own dissatisfactions with life. But never is there morbidity or sentimentality, the mind's dialogue with itself has been ruthlessly silenced.

A greater threat to the resolution than the possibility of stasis in self-pity is the desire to join the beloved in death, a something beyond reason every true griever has experienced, from the suicides (if such they be) of Pharoah Djer's tomb at Abydos and the Royal Death-pits of Ur to lovers' death-pacts, suttee, those who self-immolate at the death of an icon – and the narrator of Arnold's 'Requiescat' of 1853:

In quiet she reposes;
Ah, would that I did too!
(3-4)

Grief is so powerful an emotion because it is an unstable mix of all the others, blameful, self-pitying, vindictive, emergent at the most inappropriate time, utterly unpredictable and contradictory in its actions, terrifying, murderous, even lustful. Above all, suicidal.

Despair at earthly existence prompted Keats's "I have been half in love with easeful death" ('Ode to a Nightingale' VI, 2); despair at the world and grief for Clough prompted Arnold's:

> And strange and vain the earthly turmoil grows,
> And near and real the charm of thy repose,
> And night as welcome as a friend would fall.
>
> (148-150)

This is self-hypnosis if not necromancy – for the night that in ever-nearing circle weaves her shade (132) is casting a magical spell ("the charm of thy repose"), and reminds us of Coleridge's ecstatic prophet and the poet's injunction to us to "weave a circle round him thrice" ('Kubla Khan', 51) to ward off his awesome otherwordliness. (Coleridge's influence is also seen in the alliterative "Well! wind-dispersed and vain the words will be" (101), that echo the 'Dejection: An Ode's) opening line of "Well! If the bard was weatherwise," a poem of the instinctive joy to be had from nature when all else fails; and the stylistic influence of Milton on both may be seen in the "Well knows to still the wild winds when they roar" of his pastoral masque 'Comus'). Here the spell places Arnold outside himself – he both sees and foresees his dying youth, advancing age, his own death. But he is snapped out of his self-hypnosis by the hunters, and flees from the death that has already engulfed Clough who cannot follow him to the lonely ridge as the hunters career "adown the dusk hill-side" into hell.

Arnold emerges into the English countryside, Clough completes the underworld journey to the lucent Arno-vale of Elysium and "all the marvel of the golden skies". Separated forever, the emblematic tree is now the only link between them.

Stanzas 20 and 21 – reconciliation with death

The way from despair to reconciliation takes the reader through a bitter observation of human nature as materialistic, a market-place that links us to the city so long avoided and "the great town's harsh heart-wearying roar" at the end – and also returns us to the very start of the poem and the manner of Clough's leaving Arcadia:

Some life of men unblest
He knew, which made him droop, and fill'd his head.
                                          (46-47)

Like Keats in 'Adonais', Clough has had to bear vituperation and over-sensitivity:

Men gave thee nothing; but this happy quest,
If men esteem'd thee feeble, gave thee power,
If men procured thee trouble, gave thee rest.
                                  ('Thyrsis', 213-215)

Envy and calumny and hate and pain,
And that unrest which men miscall delight,
Can touch him not and torture not again.
                                  ('Adonais', XL, 2-4)

Lines 191-200 and 201-210 of 'Thyrsis' return us to Arnold's despair, but a despair he wilfully purges of bitterness and grief. We are back in the Berkshire landscape, but a landscape where the Scholar-Gypsy is more meaningful ("outliving thee") than Clough in Elysium, where the English countryside and "that lone, sky-pointing tree, are not for him" (174). But what does this mean? – the Scholar-Gypsy is of course a purely literary figure (as explicated in the poem of that name) that lives in each generation's imagination, and Clough takes over his role as the symbol of the search for truth, felt to be immanent in nature, as is made clear by line 211, "Thou too, O Thyrsis, on like quest wast bound" and line 230, "Left human haunt, and on alone till night." Clough is not reborn – he lives in a world of his own loving, the passionate Arcadia of his youth. But Arnold's memory of him on like quest amidst the Berkshire landscape equates him with the imaginary Scholar-Gypsy, the fleer of modernity and materialism, and sets him just as firmly in the Cumnor Hills.

Arnold is alone physically – "Sole in these fields! yet will I not despair" (192), the fields being both those of Berkshire in the present, and Phrygia and Sicily of their youth; sole (with its echo of Keats's Ruth "amidst the alien corn") because of the death of Clough; sole with its resonance of *Paradise Lost* because the past hope of the pastoral does not work in the present, for Sicily and Phrygia are not England; and sole because he is fighting a rearguard action –

classicism cannot overturn the Industrial Revolution. Yet he "will not despair" – he is resigned to death, Clough's as well as his own. Clough's memory has metamorphosed into something meaningful and the poem can move finally to its resolution.

The resolution (the narrator's apotheosis)

All the themes we have discussed lead up to and unite in the resolution, but to be emotionlly satisfying it has in terms of the pastoral elegy to be twofold – the narrator consoled and the dead friend somehow reborn. In 'Thyrsis' it is the salutary warning to Arnold that he must return to nature for mental sustenance; for Clough we are to imagine him in his Arcadian world beneath the Cumnor Hills, linked to the Berkshire countryside by his ever-youthful quest for truth. The signal-elm contains within its single unity the various strands of these resolutions: its boughs touch the "marvel of the golden skies," its bole is blossoming on the Berkshire hill of their youth, and its roots reach deep into Proserpine's Sicilian fields with their "immortal chants of old"

But as for Arnold, where is his consolation? How exactly does Clough live on? – Certainly as no literary trope or nebulous symbol; like the Scholar-Gypsy of old he has become Arnold's intellectual conscience.

> Let in thy voice a whisper often come,
>   To chase fatigue and fear.
>   (235-236)

He has become Arnold's constant reminder that the urban turmoil contains no answer to any universal question, let alone ease from the pangs of existence, for with the advent of Manchester the city no longer symbolised man but man the city. Clough has become our exhorter to flee the city for nature, for nature whether it be ancient Sicily or modern Berkshire holds in herself, in her unchanging renewal, the answer to change itself. And amongst the Cumnor Hills she expresses herself as the scholar-gypsy, as Clough strewing amongst the fields and denes the coronals – spiritual as well as physical – of her return, for like Bion in Moschus' 'Lament for Bion' (125) Proserpina has given the poet back unto the hills. Ancient faith and present reality become reconciled. Arcadia lies reachable under

Cumnor, classicism overgrown by – but graspable through – modern sentiment; old change analysed by new change and Clough reborn is their referential symbol:

> Dost thou ask proof? Our tree yet crowns the hill,
> Our Scholar travels yet the loved hill-side.
>
> (239-240)

This is the narrator's apotheosis, the divine sign that requires a change in his attitude to Clough's demise – for a moment he has risen above death and become, like the renaissance gnostics, divinely detached in his ability to appreciate its necessity in the cycle of life, to understand before the poem returns to the hillside of its beginning the branch-to-root interconnectedness of everything.

On the hottest day of 1998 I followed their path to where the elm-tree once had stood, and – if only for an indulgent moment – imagined as I gazed over Matthew Arnold's Field (bought by public subscription) towards the Vale of White Horse, that all who had ever delighted in this countryside had left a part of their wonder breathing through it, drawing us into a perpetual search of its mystery.

'Thyrsis' reaffirms that the pastoral elegy is no outdated form that serves merely as an excavation site for art-archaeologists – every great poet has added his own genius to it. The lack of overt Christian reference in the poem may have its cause in Arnold's agnosticism, but its absence marks a profound shift in the pastoral elegy's millenia-long movement, from Adonis as saviour to Christ as saviour, through Christ as saviour to 'Thyrsis' and man his own saviour. Suddenly alone amidst the monuments of his spiritual destruction, he is weakly dependant on his own intellectuality to conquer grief and glimpse some meaning to an existence without God and a death without resurrection. 'Thyrsis', in its appeal to and rejection of the classical, is the last pastoral elegy to the divine and the first to modern humanism.

The ritual purging of death has proved its worth in life and literature from 'Gilgamesh' to our own times, and even its cynical reversal of values by Eliot has merely strengthened its tenacity and adaptability. I hope I have conveyed – and passed on – to the reader my love of the form and 'Thyrsis' in particular, and like the spirit of Clough I exhort them to to go back to the internal landscape of the

154

poem and explore the many aspects that shortage of space has forced me to pass over – its stylistic and rhythmic qualities (not perfect in parts), the application of Parnassianism, the literary debt to Clough's poetry, the poem's Berkeleyan and Stoic elements, comparison with 'In Memoriam' (that other contemporary monument to the death of a youthful friend and poet) – and of course Arnold's flying in the face of his own poetic theory, for when he did so his greatest poetry emerged.

Bibliography

Years ago at university I had to write a critique of Thomas Mann's *Death in Venice*, quoting any sources I had used. After finishing what I thought was a highly original piece of work I proudly wrote at the end "No sources", to which my tutor added after I had submitted it: "What! – have you never read a book?" The unconscious sources of this essay are legion and my debt to forgotten lectures, old teachers, rapidly scanned reviews, passing arguments with friends of long ago and erudite books I didn't even know I owned must be beyond payment. Unforgotten, however, are Professor Whitney F. Bolton and Dr Ian Fletcher, formerly of Reading University, for their teaching on Old English and Milton respectively. The bibliographical sources I am consciously – if at times only fleetingly – indebted to, I list below.

Life
Lang, C.L. *The Letters of Matthew Arnold* (2 Vols.) (University Press of Virginia, 1996)
Murray, N. *A Life of Matthew Arnold*, (London, 1996)
Trilling, L. *Matthew Arnold*, (London, 1939)

Works and criticisms
Anderson, W.D. *Arnold and the Classical Tradition*, (London, 1965)
Annan, N. *Matthew Arnold Selected Essays*, (The World's Classics), (OUP, 1964)
Arnold, M. *Irish Essays and Others*, (London, 1891)
Arnold, M. *Discourses in America*, (London, 1889)
Arnold – Poetical Works (Eds. C.B. Tinker and H.F. Lowry), (OUP, 1950) (repr.1969)

Arnold – Poems Selected by Kenneth Allott (The Penguin Poetry Library), (London, 1954) (repr.1985)

Buckler, W.E. *On the Poetry of Matthew Arnold: Essays in Critical Reconstruction*, (New York University Press, 1982)

Collini, S. *Culture and Anarchy and Other Writings* (Ed.) (CUP, 1993)

Eliot, T.S. *Arnold and Pater* (*Selected Essays*), (London, 1932)

Eliot, T.S. *Matthew Arnold* (*The Use of Poetry and the Use of Criticism*), (London, 1933)

Leavis, F.R. *Arnold as Critic* (Scrutiny VII), (1938)

Livingston, J.C. *Matthew Arnold and Christianity: His Religious Prose Writings*, (University of South Carolina Press, 1986)

Machann, C. *Matthew Arnold: A Literary Life*, (St Martin's Press Inc., 1998)

Matthew Arnold – Dover Beach and other Poems, Dover Thrift Editions (Volume Editor: Candace Ward), (New York, 1994)

Rowse, A.L. *Matthew Arnold: Poet and Prophet*, (University Press of America, 1986)

Schneider, M.W. *Poetry in the Age of Democracy: The Literary Criticism of Matthew Arnold*, (University Press of Kansas, 1989)

Selected Poems: Matthew Arnold (Ed. S.P. Sen Gupta), (Calcutta, 1979)

Trilling, L. *Matthew Arnold*, (London, 1949)

Wilson, J. Dover *Culture and Anarchy by Matthew Arnold* (Landmarks in the History of Education), (CUP, 1960)

General
Baker, M. *Discovering the Folklore of Plants*, (Princes Risborough, 1966)

Briggs, A. *Victorian Cities*, (London, 1963)

Edmonds, J.M. *The Greek Bucolic Poets* (Loeb Classical Library), (London, 1919)

Engels, F. *The Condition of the Working Class in England*, (London, 1892) (repr. 1974)

Frye, N. *Anatomy of Criticism*, (Princeton, 1957)

George, A. *The Epic of Gilgamesh*, (London, 1999)

Herbert, K. *Looking for the Lost Gods of England*, (London, 1994)

Highet, G. *The Classical Tradition*, (Oxford, 1957) (repr. 1967)

Hopkirk, P. *The Great Game*, (London, 1990)

James, E.O. *Comparative Religion*, (London, 1938) (rev. 1961)

Keanie, A. *William Wordsworth* (Greenwich Exchange Student Guides), (London, 2000)

Lord, A.B. *The Singer of Tales*, (Cambridge, Massachusetts, 1960)

Lucas, F.L. *The Decline and Fall of the Romantic Ideal*, (Cambridge, 1936) (repr. 1963)

Ricks, C. *Milton's Grand Style*, (Oxford, 1963)

Rieu, E. *Homer – The Odyssey*, (Penguin Classics), (London, 1950) (repr.1968)

Shippey, T.A. *Old English Verse*, (London, 1972)

Wells, R. *The Idylls – Theocritus*, (Penguin Classics), (London, 1989)

West, D. *Virgil – The Aeneid*, (Penguin Classics), (London, 1991)

Maps

Pathfinder 1116: *Oxford* (Ordnance Survey 1:25,000), Southampton, 1992

Landranger 164: *Oxford & surrounding area* (Ordnance Survey 1:50,000), Southampton, 1993

Readers who wish to comment on – or query – any aspect of this essay may contact me by e-mail courtesy of the publisher at greenx01@globalnet.co.uk though I cannot guarantee an answer in every case.

Index

GREENWICH EXCHANGE BOOKS

Greenwich Exchange Student Guides are critical studies of major or contemporary serious writers in English and selected European languages. The series is for the student, the teacher and 'common readers' and is an ideal resource for libraries. The *Times Educational Supplement* praised these books, saying, "The style of these guides has a pressure of meaning behind it. Students should learn from that ... If art is about selection, perception and taste, then this is it."

(ISBN prefix 1-871551- applies)
The series includes:
W.H. Auden by Stephen Wade (36-6)
Honoré de Balzac by Wendy Mercer (48-X)
William Blake by Peter Davies (27-7)
The Brontës by Peter Davies (24-2)
Robert Browning by John Lucas (59-5)
Samuel Taylor Coleridge by Andrew Keanie (64-1)
Joseph Conrad by Martin Seymour-Smith (18-8)
William Cowper by Michael Thorn (25-0)
Charles Dickens by Robert Giddings (26-9)
Emily Dickinson by Marnie Pomeroy (68-4)
John Donne by Sean Haldane (23-4)
Ford Madox Ford by Anthony Fowles (63-3)
The Stagecraft of Brian Friel by David Grant (74-9)
Robert Frost by Warren Hope (70-6)
Thomas Hardy by Sean Haldane (33-1)
Seamus Heaney by Warren Hope (37-4)
Gerard Manley Hopkins by Sean Sheehan (77-3)
James Joyce by Michael Murphy (73-0)
Philip Larkin by Warren Hope (35-8)
Poets of the First World War by John Greening (79-X)
Laughter in the Dark – The Plays of Joe Orton by Arthur Burke (56-0)
Philip Roth by Paul McDonald (72-2)
Shakespeare's *Macbeth* by Matt Simpson (69-2)
Shakespeare's *Othello* by Matt Simpson (71-4)
Shakespeare's *The Tempest* by Matt Simpson (75-7)
Shakespeare's Non-Dramatic Poetry by Martin Seymour-Smith (22-6)
Shakespeare's Sonnets by Martin Seymour-Smith (38-2)
Tobias Smollett by Robert Giddings (21-8)
Dylan Thomas by Peter Davies (78-1)
Alfred, Lord Tennyson by Michael Thorn (20-X)
William Wordsworth by Andrew Keanie (57-9)

176

OTHER GREENWICH EXCHANGE BOOKS
Paperback unless otherwise stated.

LITERATURE & BIOGRAPHY

Aleister Crowley and the Cult of Pan *by Paul Newman*
Few more nightmarish figures stalk English literature than Aleister Crowley
(1875-1947), poet, magician, mountaineer and agent provocateur. In this
groundbreaking study, Paul Newman dives into the occult mire of Crowley's
works and fishes out gems and grotesqueries that are by turns ethereal,
sublime, pornographic and horrifying. An influential exponent of the cult
of the Great God Pan, his essentially 'pagan' outlook was shared by major
European writers as well as English novelists like E.M. Forster, D.H.
Lawrence and Arthur Machen.
Paul Newman lives in Cornwall. Editor of the literary magazine *Abraxas*,
he has written over ten books.
2004 • 223 pages • ISBN 1-871551-66-8

The Author, the Book and the Reader *by Robert Giddings*
This collection of essays analyses the effects of changing technology and
the attendant commercial pressures on literary styles and subject matter.
Authors covered include Charles Dickens, Tobias George Smollett, Mark
Twain, Dr Johnson and John le Carré.
1991 • 220 pages • illustrated • ISBN 1-871551-01-3

John Dryden *by Anthony Fowles*
Of all the poets of the Augustan age, John Dryden was the most worldly.
Anthony Fowles traces Dryden's evolution from 'wordsmith' to major poet.
This critical study shows a poet of vigour and technical panache whose art
was forged in the heat and battle of a turbulent polemical and pamphleteering
age. Although Dryden's status as a literary critic has long been established,
Fowles draws attention to Dryden's neglected achievements as a translator
of poetry. He deals also with the less well-known aspects of Dryden's work
– his plays and occasional pieces.
Anthony Fowles was born in London and educated at the Universities of
Oxford and Southern California. He began his career in filmmaking before
becoming an author of film and television scripts and more than twenty
books.
2003 • 292 pages • ISBN 1-871551-58-7

The Good That We Do *by John Lucas*
John Lucas' book blends fiction, biography and social history in order to tell the story of his grandfather, Horace Kelly. Headteacher of a succession of elementary schools in impoverished areas of London, 'Hod' Kelly was also a keen cricketer, a devotee of the music hall, and included among his friends the great Trade Union leader, Ernest Bevin. In telling the story of his life, Lucas has provided a fascinating range of insights into the lives of ordinary Londoners from the First World War until the outbreak of the Second World War. Threaded throughout is an account of such people's hunger for education, and of the different ways government, church and educational officialdom ministered to that hunger. *The Good That We Do* is both a study of one man and of a period when England changed, drastically and forever.
John Lucas is Professor of English at Nottingham Trent University and is a poet and critic.
2001 • 214 pages • ISBN 1-871551-54-4

In Pursuit of Lewis Carroll *by Raphael Shaberman*
Sherlock Holmes and the author uncover new evidence in their investigations into the mysterious life and writing of Lewis Carroll. They examine published works by Carroll that have been overlooked by previous commentators. A newly discovered poem, almost certainly by Carroll, is published here.
Amongst many aspects of Carroll's highly complex personality, this book explores his relationship with his parents, numerous child friends, and the formidable Mrs Liddell, mother of the immortal Alice. Raphael Shaberman was a founder member of the Lewis Carroll Society and a teacher of autistic children.
1994 • 118 pages • illustrated • ISBN 1-871551-13-7

Liar! Liar!: Jack Kerouac – Novelist *by R.J. Ellis*
The fullest study of Jack Kerouac's fiction to date. It is the first book to devote an individual chapter to every one of his novels. *On the Road, Visions of Cody* and *The Subterraneans* are reread in-depth, in a new and exciting way. *Visions of Gerard* and *Doctor Sax* are also strikingly reinterpreted, as are other daringly innovative writings, like 'The Railroad Earth' and his "try at a spontaneous *Finnegans Wake*" – *Old Angel Midnight*. Neglected writings, such as *Tristessa* and *Big Sur*, are also analysed, alongside better-known novels such as *Dharma Bums* and *Desolation Angels*.
R.J. Ellis is Senior Lecturer in English at Nottingham Trent University.
1999 • 295 pages • ISBN 1-871551-53-6

Musical Offering *by Yolanthe Leigh*

In a series of vivid sketches, anecdotes and reflections, Yolanthe Leigh tells the story of her growing up in the Poland of the 1930s and the Second World War. These are poignant episodes of a child's first encounters with both the enchantments and the cruelties of the world; and from a later time, stark memories of the brutality of the Nazi invasion, and the hardships of student life in Warsaw under the Occupation. But most of all this is a record of inward development; passages of remarkable intensity and simplicity describe the girl's response to religion, to music, and to her discovery of philosophy.

Yolanthe Leigh was formerly a Lecturer in Philosophy at Reading University.

2000 • 57 pages • ISBN: 1-871551-46-3

Norman Cameron *by Warren Hope*

Norman Cameron's poetry was admired by W.H. Auden, celebrated by Dylan Thomas and valued by Robert Graves. He was described by Martin Seymour-Smith as, "one of ... the most rewarding and pure poets of his generation ..." and is at last given a full length biography. This eminently sociable man, who had periods of darkness and despair, wrote little poetry by comparison with others of his time, but always of a consistently high quality – imaginative and profound.

2000 • 221 pages • illustrated • ISBN 1-871551-05-6

Poetry in Exile *by Michael Murphy*

"Michael Murphy discriminates the forms of exile and expatriation with the shrewdness of the cultural historian, the acuity of the literary critic, and the subtlety of a poet alert to the ways language and poetic form embody the precise contours of experience. His accounts of Auden, Brodsky and Szirtes not only cast much new light on the work of these complex and rewarding poets, but are themselves a pleasure to read." *Stan Smith, Research Professor in Literary Studies, Nottingham Trent University*

"In this brilliant book Murphy strives to get at the essence of 'poetry in exile' itself and to explain how it is at the centre of the whole political and cultural experience of the turbulent 20th century. His critical insight makes it one of the most important recent books on poetry in English." *Bernard O'Donoghue, Wadham College, Oxford*

Michael Murphy teaches English Literature at Liverpool Hope University College.

2004 • 268 pages • ISBN 1-871551-76-5

POETRY

Adam's Thoughts in Winter *by Warren Hope*
Warren Hope's poems have appeared from time to time in a number of literary periodicals, pamphlets and anthologies on both sides of the Atlantic. They appeal to lovers of poetry everywhere. His poems are brief, clear, frequently lyrical, characterised by wit, but often distinguished by tenderness. The poems gathered in this first book-length collection counter the brutalising ethos of contemporary life, speaking of and for the virtues of modesty, honesty and gentleness in an individual, memorable way.
2000 • 47 pages • ISBN 1-871551-40-4

Baudelaire: Les Fleurs du Mal *Translated by F.W. Leakey*
Selected poems from *Les Fleurs du Mal* are translated with parallel French texts and are designed to be read with pleasure by readers who have no French as well as those who are practised in the French language.
F.W. Leakey was Professor of French in the University of London. As a scholar, critic and teacher he specialised in the work of Baudelaire for 50 years and published a number of books on the poet.
2001 • 153 pages • ISBN 1-871551-10-2

'The Last Blackbird' and other poems by Ralph Hodgson *edited and introduced by John Harding*
Ralph Hodgson (1871-1962) was a poet and illustrator whose most influentialand enduring work appeared to great acclaim just prior to and during the First World War. His work is imbued with a spiritual passion for the beauty of creation and the mystery of existence. This new selection brings together, for the first time in 40 years, some of the most beautiful and powerful 'hymns to life' in the English language.
John Harding lives in London. He is a freelance writer and teacher and is Ralph Hodgson's biographer.
2004 • 70 pages • ISBN 1-871551-81-1

Lines from the Stone Age *by Sean Haldane*
Reviewing Sean Haldane's 1992 volume *Desire in Belfast*, Robert Nye wrote in *The Times* that "Haldane can be sure of his place among the English poets." This place is not yet a conspicuous one, mainly because his early volumes appeared in Canada and because he has earned his living by other means than literature. Despite this, his poems have always had their circle of readers. The 60 previously unpublished poems of *Lines from the Stone Age* – "lines of longing, terror, pride, lust and pain" – may widen this circle.
2000 • 53 pages • ISBN 1-871551-39-0

Shakespeare's Sonnets *by Martin Seymour-Smith*
Martin Seymour-Smith's outstanding achievement lies in the field of literary biography and criticism. In 1963 he produced his comprehensive edition, in the old spelling, of *Shakespeare's Sonnets* (here revised and corrected by himself and Peter Davies in 1998). With its landmark introduction and its brilliant critical commentary on each sonnet, it was praised by William Empson and John Dover Wilson. Stephen Spender said of him "I greatly admire Martin Seymour-Smith for the independence of his views and the great interest of his mind"; and both Robert Graves and Anthony Burgess described him as the leading critic of his time. His exegesis of the *Sonnets* remains unsurpassed.
2001 • 194 pages • ISBN 1-871551-38-2

Wilderness *by Martin Seymour-Smith*
This is Martin Seymour-Smith's first publication of his poetry for more than twenty years. This collection of 36 poems is a fearless account of an inner life of love, frustration, guilt, laughter and the celebration of others. He is best known to the general public as the author of the controversial and bestselling *Hardy* (1994).
1994 • 52 pages • ISBN 1-871551-08-0

BUSINESS

English Language Skills *by Vera Hughes*
If you want to be sure, (as a student, or in your business or personal life), that your written English is correct, this book is for you. Vera Hughes' aim is to help you remember the basic rules of spelling, grammar and punctuation. 'Noun', 'verb', 'subject', 'object' and 'adjective' are the only technical terms used. The book teaches the clear, accurate English required by the business and office world. It coaches acceptable current usage and makes the rules easier to remember.
Vera Hughes was a civil servant and is a trainer and author of training manuals.
2002 • 142 pages • ISBN 1-871551-60-9